CONSCIENCE OF A CONSERVATIVE

JEFF FLAKE

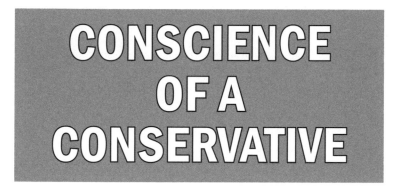

CONSCIENCE OF A CONSERVATIVE

★ ★ ★

RANDOM HOUSE

NEW YORK

Published in the United States by Random House,
an imprint and division of Penguin Random House LLC, New York.

RANDOM HOUSE and the HOUSE colophon are
registered trademarks of Penguin Random House LLC.

Hardback ISBN 9780399592911
Ebook ISBN 9780399592928

Printed in the United States of America on acid-free paper

randomhousebooks.com

2 4 6 8 9 7 5 3 1

FIRST EDITION

*To that girl I met
on a faraway beach
so long ago*

The conscience of the Conservative is pricked by *anyone* who
would debase the dignity of the individual human being.
Today, therefore, he is at odds with dictators who rule
by terror, and equally with those gentler collectivists
who ask our permission to play God
with the human race.

—BARRY GOLDWATER,
The Conscience of a Conservative, 1960

TO STAND ALONE

I WILL START BY SAYING that I regret having to write this book.

I regret it because its necessity is a sign that the American conservative movement, which has been a force for great good to our country and to the world, is lost. This book aims to describe how it went wrong, and why, and how it might correct course. Given the state of our politics, it is no exaggeration to say that this is an urgent matter.

Conservatives can hold no one else responsible for this. It is a crisis of our own making. The good news is that fixing American conservatism is both of vital importance to our civic well-being and eminently achievable. But to do so, we have to be honest about what has happened.

I am a committed conservative. That means that I believe in the power of conservative principles to transform lives, lift countries, alleviate suffering, and make people prosperous and free. I strongly believe that given the choice between free markets and free minds versus more government control over our lives, the United States will almost always choose the conservative path.

But the question has become: Will "conservatives" choose the conservative path? Or will we instead sacrifice principle to do what is easiest and most politically expedient? When it comes to the election of 2016, well, we already have the answers. As conservative principle retreated, something new and troubling took its place. Going forward, those questions remain open, the answers remain unclear, and the early signs are troubling.

I grew up on a cattle ranch in northern Arizona, where conditions were spartan and life was what you made it. That experience taught me the value of standing alone sometimes, and it has everything to do with why I am now writing this book. And for the ultimate example in standing alone, we conservatives owe a great debt to a towering figure from Arizona, Senator Barry Goldwater, who more than fifty years ago stood alone when it was extremely difficult to do so, and in so doing started a movement of conservatives that twenty years later would see the election of one of our greatest presidents, Ronald Reagan. That this book takes its name from Senator Goldwater's seminal book is an homage to both his fierce independence and his visionary leadership.

Goldwater's fight was for the soul of the country, and so, too, is ours. When he wrote this in his own time, he may as well have been writing it in ours: "Though we Conservatives are deeply persuaded that our society is ailing, and know that Conservatism holds the key to national salvation—and feel sure the country agrees with us—we seem unable to demonstrate the practical relevance of Conservative principles to the needs of the day."

The effect that Goldwater had on my state and on the way that Americans think about their relationship to their government cannot be overstated. It is our relationship to our government and the foundational institutions of American liberty that are now under severe stress.

That conservatism has become compromised by other powerful forces—nationalism, populism, xenophobia, extreme partisanship, even celebrity—explains part of how and why we lost our way. That we who call ourselves conservative have been willing partners in that compromise explains the rest.

It doesn't have to be this way. In fact, it simply cannot be this way.

Going forward from here, for Americans to have the benefit of conservative principles, we must once again have the benefit of truly conservative leadership. Unabashed, unafraid, unreserved conservative leadership. But almost two decades into the new century, we conservatives have suffered a crisis of confidence, which in turn has led to a crisis of principle. In the election campaign of 2016, it was as if we no longer had the courage of our convictions and so chose to simply abandon conviction altogether, taking up instead an unfamiliar banner and a new set of values that had never been our own.

That an enigmatic Republican nominee succeeded in becoming president resolves nothing in terms of the future of American conservatism. In fact, an enigma by definition is a riddle, and riddles are meant to be solved. We—as conservatives and as Americans—have a lot of solving to do, to restore principle and look to the future.

Politicians can be herdlike creatures, too often prone to taking the path of least resistance. I understand the impulse and have often sought that well-trodden path myself. I must say, it would have been much easier for me to have taken that path this time as well and fallen in line with most in my party. But in good conscience, I could not. The stakes, for the future of conservatism and for the future of our country, are simply too high.

CONTENTS

CONSCIENCE OF A CONSERVATIVE

CHAPTER ONE

THE CRISIS
WE FACE

FOR THREE STRAIGHT DAYS in October 1969, at the peak of both the Vietnam War and our tensions with the Soviet Union, the United States military was secretly placed on full war readiness around the globe, and bombers armed with nuclear weapons flew patterns close to Soviet airspace. The Nixon administration let the Soviets know, via diplomatic channels, that "the madman was loose," meaning that it was impossible to say what President Nixon might do next.

At approximately the same time, Nixon told his chief of staff, Bob Haldeman: "I want the North Vietnamese to believe that I've reached the point that I might do anything to stop the war. We'll just slip the word to them that . . . 'you know Nixon is obsessed about communism. We can't restrain him when he is angry—and he has his hand on the nuclear button'—Ho Chi Minh himself will be in Paris in two days begging for peace."

Nixon believed that there can be value in being unpredictable. If your adversaries don't know what you're going to do or how you'll react, you may be able to establish a strategic advantage over them and elicit a better response in a given situation than if your response is predictable or preordained. Another power, not wanting to test such unpredictability, might then forego territorial ambitions or think twice about causing trouble in its own sphere of influence.

This theory of unpredictability, dubbed the "madman theory," assumes a strategy underlying the unpredictability. Absent strategy, we are left with no theory, just the madman. Or, more to the point, we are left with erratic behavior in the highest office, which is not a virtue in foreign policy—or in any policy, really.

Erratic behavior, unmoored from principle, is the opposite of conservatism, which is, I believe, the animating idea of government and its relationship to the governed as established by our Founders—that government should be limited and prudent in its exercise of the power granted it by the people. It is these principles that I was schooled in and that inspire and humble me every day.

In short, there is a significant difference between *appearing* to have problems with impulse control and *actually having* impulse-control problems. And so in our own time, in a very different presidency, we would do well to examine anew the efficacy of unpredictability.

On December 2, 2016, at 7:44 P.M., not quite a month after he was elected president, President-Elect Donald J. Trump tweeted this message to his followers: "The President of Taiwan CALLED ME today to wish me congratulations on winning the Presidency. Thank you!"

The 104 characters described a diplomatic breach, after which a firestorm had erupted. Trump's first tweet was followed at 8:41 P.M. with this: "Interesting how the U.S. sells Taiwan billions of dollars of military equipment but I should not accept a congratulatory call."

The context for Trump's tweets is that that same morning, upsetting the "One China" protocol that had been observed by six American presidents from both parties since 1979, Trump had taken a phone call from the president of Taiwan, risking our relationship with Beijing, which is precarious under the best of circumstances. Foreign policy experts across the ideological spectrum were aghast—the established kabuki theater of international diplomacy and stability had been violated, and flagrantly so. For anyone who pays attention to these matters, the breach was a big deal.

For my part, I will say that overreaction seems to be the order of the day (and perhaps the desired effect) when it comes to all things to do with Donald Trump, and that the sky did not fall after the president-elect's chat with Taiwanese president Tsai Ing-wen. At least it hasn't yet. I will also say that it may even be past time to consider a change—in a nuanced way—in our relationship with China and Taiwan, if that change is pursued purposefully.

But in the tweeting life of our president, strategy is difficult to detect. Influencing the news cycles seems to be the principal goal; achieving short-term tactical advantage, you bet. But ultimately, it's all noise and no signal. And in the absence of preparation and a well-considered strategy—especially when one is moving global chess pieces—volatile unpredictability is not a virtue. We have quite enough volatile actors to deal with internationally as it is without becoming one of them.

Of course, I could be wrong about the president's seeming lack of strategy in Taiwan or on other matters, and because he is my president and as an American I fervently wish him to succeed, I have been more than willing to give him the benefit of the doubt. Particularly because I so trust and admire his national security team, Defense Secretary James Mattis and—since the removal of the conspiracy theorist Michael Flynn—National Security Advisor H. R. McMaster.

In any case, the Chinese government, dismissing the breach of protocol as a "small trick," seemed to take it all in stride. So maybe Mr. Trump's gambit was both strategic and successful after all.

But it is one thing to seek to keep your global adversaries or "near-peer competitors" off-balance with strategic unpredictability and quite another to keep the American people themselves similarly at a loss as to what exactly is going on, which is now a daily occurrence, to say nothing at all about the vexation on the part of our many traditional allies all over the world.

I began writing this book after returning from a trip to Mexico City on a one-senator diplomatic mission to calm and reassure the nation to our south—a vitally important friend and trading partner—that all will be well, that America is still America. But is it?

The meetings with Mexican officials were planned before the election, but they took on greater significance after Trump's win. But even before the election, it was obvious that my party had taken a sharp turn away from the conservative principles that have defined it for nearly a century and that I have tried to uphold for my entire life. And the animating question of how this had happened to my party seemed already to be a profound problem for our democracy, one badly in need of a solution.

I write this book because we as conservatives—and conservatism itself—are in crisis.

On its face, that might seem a preposterous claim, given that the American political party most closely and most often associated with conservatism currently occupies the White House and controls both houses of Congress. But make no mistake, as a governing philosophy, conservatism is indeed in crisis—and not in spite of this apparent success but because of it.

Let me explain.

In terms of global ideological struggle, we conservatives have since the Second World War feared and prepared for the rise of left-wing governments in Europe, and as part of this vigilance, we have relentlessly and with justification sought to curb the excesses of liberalism in the United States. After all, the health of our system depends on two healthy governing parties, and our role in striking this balance has been to keep a check on the power of the government. In this endeavor, our results have been decidedly mixed. Since the early twentieth century, the size and scope of the government of the United States has experienced explosive growth by every metric—particularly since the New Deal, during which much of our current social welfare and regulatory institutions were conceived, giving government a greater and greater share of control over the lives of individuals. Call it the First Law of Political Thermodynamics: Governments Grow. Such growth has made the job of the conservative all the more necessary, and all the more urgent, to fight this encroachment with everything we've got.

That remains the right fight for conservatives, but we must always be strong enough to look honestly at ourselves, too. Liberals have much to answer for for the role they've played in achieving our current dysfunction, but I will let liberals take care of themselves. Because all political actors are also fallible mortals, we—the conservative part of our polity—also have excesses and extremes, our own worst impulses to keep in check. That is the subject of this book.

How is it that the Republican Party, the political movement that has long been animated by the simple, strong ideas of limited government and economic freedom, has been swept up in a populist fever and has fallen for ideas that are the opposite of what so many of us have believed for so long—from ardent belief in free trade to realpolitik federal budgeting to responsible immigration policy to making the Republican Party as big a tent as possible—all united by a belief that, as George Will once wrote, "limited government *by its limitations* nurtures in men and women the responsibilities that make them competent for, and worthy of, freedom"?

By any honest assessment of where we are as a party, without a major course correction, we are simply on the way out. The demographic picture of America is rapidly changing, and we have to change with it. George W. Bush got 56 percent of the white vote, and won. Mitt Romney got 59 percent of the white vote, and lost. Every four years in this country, the electorate gets about two percentage points less white; as an increasingly old and increasingly white party, we are skidding with each passing election toward irrelevance in terms of appealing to a broad electorate. We hold out our hand, expecting our share of nonwhite votes, and yet we give these Americans too few reasons to come our way. Instead, we demonize them, marginalize them, blame them for our country's problems. We knew all of this before the last election, but we quickly set it aside for the sugar high of populism, nativism, and demagoguery. The crash from this sugar high will be particularly unpleasant.

But it's deeper than that. We have given in to the politics of anger—the belief that riling up the base can make up for failed attempts to broaden the electorate. These are the spasms of a dying party. Anger and resentment and blaming groups of people for our problems might work politically in the short term, but it's a dangerous impulse in a pluralistic society, and we know from history that it's an impulse that, once acted upon, never ends well.

I had hoped before the last election that we would salvage our party and actually learn and act on the lessons from the famous "autopsy" that the Republican Party issued after Mitt Romney's unsuccessful presidential run in 2012, which set forth a program of how to grow and be a relevant and dynamic part of a rapidly changing America. We would once again be the party animated by ideas and not ire. But we instead took a step closer to the apocalyptic brink by becoming a party that calls for the jailing of its political opponents.

This problem, of course, has been a long time coming. I remember when we were the party of ideas. I still have a T-shirt from the early 1990s, commemorating the barnstorming battle royale national tour taken by two Texas Republican congressmen—Dick Armey and Bill Archer—selling out lecture halls to debate the benefits of a national flat tax versus a national consumption tax. I was back home in Arizona then, running a think tank called the Goldwater Institute, and I lived for these kinds of debates, with large and consequential ideas. Even the Contract with America, which was advanced by another character with extraordinary talents for self-promotion, Newt Gingrich, was issues-based. Some of the Institute's patrons would regularly urge me to turn the Institute over to more hot-button social issues, but politically those issues could be terribly destructive and divisive, as they were often only intended as the bases for culture wars, so—with the libertarian western senator whose name the Institute proudly bore always in the back of my mind—I resisted. Give me the great economic thinkers and arguments, because that is where the Institute can make a difference. The issues that increase freedom and broaden opportunity for the most people are the issues that I wanted to devote my energies to.

It's funny: At the same time that I was executive director of the Goldwater Institute in Arizona, Mike Pence was doing the same thing at the Indiana Policy Review, another free-market think tank. We were elected to Congress the same year—2000—just in time to watch President Bush push through No Child Left Behind and the Medicare Part D prescription drug benefit, programs that were absolutely anathema to think-tank Republicans. We were sitting on the House floor one day, and Mike joked that we were like Minutemen who had finally arrived at the battlefront only to be told that the revolution was over. We were desperate to engage big ideas, in a setting of intellectual curiosity and vigorous debate. I kept that Armey-Archer T-shirt so that I could remember a time when Republicans thought about ideas and enjoyed those good-spirited and consequential debates. It seems that time is gone, replaced by a race to the bottom to see who can be meaner and madder and crazier.

It is not enough to be conservative anymore. You have to be vicious. Of course, this culture of vicious dehumanization is bipartisan. But in the election of 2016, our side outdid itself. It helps if you ascribe the absolute worst motives to your opponents, traffic in outlandish conspiracy theories, abandon reason and any old-fashioned notions of the common good, and have an unquenchable appetite for destruction. But Donald Trump is not the source code for our obsession with the politics of personal destruction.

Our crisis has many fathers. Among them is Newt Gingrich, the modern progenitor of that school of politics. Any honest accounting of how we got to this new day has to reckon with Newt, whose talent for politics exceeded his interest in governing. I arrived in Congress after Gingrich departed, but I did serve with his consigliere, Tom DeLay. I remember when he gave his farewell address in the well of the House in 2006. It was DeLay who most embodied the coarse turn that politics had taken under Gingrich. DeLay was a consummate ends-justify-the-means tough guy, who by then was under indictment for his troubles.

I had arrived back at the Capitol Building straight from a family beach vacation, and on the plane I had spent nearly an hour in the cramped bathroom trying to dislodge a piece of sand that had hitched a ride in my left eye. As DeLay gave his resignation speech on the House floor, I worried that an observant reporter might mistake my moistened and still-red left eye for remorse over my role in hastening DeLay's departure from Congress. After more than five years in Congress I had my share of regrets, but doing my part in helping Tom DeLay draw a premature congressional pension wasn't one of them. His speech on the House floor confirmed my conclusion.

DeLay began by noting that there are three ways to end political careers: death, defeat, or retirement. He was happy, he said, "to bid farewell to this House under the happiest of the available options." It was a good line, though the Democrats present when his speech was given—many skipped the speech entirely, and others walked out in the middle—would accurately argue that DeLay's retirement had been prompted by his knowledge of imminent defeat in November.

From there, DeLay spoke for a defiant twenty minutes, which he described as a defense of principled partisanship. It was a powerful speech, well crafted, and for DeLay, who was not known to be an eloquent speaker, well delivered. It just wasn't believable.

"You show me a nation without partisanship, and I'll show you a tyranny," DeLay intoned. He's right. Principled partisanship is good. Compromise for the sake of compromise is no virtue. The worst legislation we pass in Congress, whether it's a silly suspension bill honoring Dairy Goat Awareness Week or a bloated appropriation bill, flies through the People's House and the world's greatest deliberative body with little dissent. But the truth is that DeLay wasn't known for political principles. Rather, he engaged in petty partisanship and the raw exercise of power. If there was a choice between passing legislation with a mix of Democratic and Republican support or passing legislation along party lines, DeLay, ever mindful of the next political ad campaign, seemed instinctively to opt for the latter.

Arguments over levels of spending have long provided a natural gulf between the parties. But as Republicans have adopted the free-spending habits of Democrats, we have been forced to exploit other areas of disagreement for petty partisan advantage. Rather than debate the future of Social Security, for example, we nearly come to blows over flag burning. The Schiavo family's horrible anguish over how do deal with the fate of their gravely ill daughter became one more set piece in Tom DeLay's political theater. One more cudgel to pound Democrats with.

What ultimately led to Tom DeLay's fall, however, was not petty partisanship but rather the standard operating procedure he advanced that was tossed around a great deal during the 2016 presidential campaign: "pay to play." One of our most cherished rights as Americans, enshrined in the First Amendment, is the right to "petition the government for a redress of grievances." The practice of lobbying is not just protected, it is a noble pursuit.

Under the "K Street Project," though, DeLay became the gatekeeper to the legislative process, and the price of admission for lobbyists was essentially to employ more Republican staffers (in many cases, former DeLay staffers) and to contribute to Republican political action committees and pet projects. It must be noted that it is we, the Republicans, who were pioneers of pay-to-play politics as much as anyone else.

In his speech, DeLay told of a nostalgic trip to the Lincoln Memorial he had recently taken, where he noted that Lincoln "keeps one of his hands in a perpetual fist." The inference DeLay wanted us to draw, of course, was that his own pugnacious nature had a noble pedigree. But with DeLay leaving Congress prematurely in an attempt to escape the verdict of both the courts and the voters, I couldn't help but think that Lincoln would use that clenched fist to punch DeLay in the nose for making the comparison.

The Party of Lincoln would now likely be unrecognizable to the Great Emancipator.

After DeLay, we Republicans went into the 2006 midterms

and got clobbered. We lost the majority in both houses, and we lost the presidency two years later and were relegated to a deep minority status. Remember, the "drain the swamp" motto that the Trump campaign took to using in the campaign of 2016 was first used by Nancy Pelosi in 2006—and for good reason. That was the earmark era, when legislative corruption spiraled out of control, and we were the biggest bottom feeders in the swamp. (I am proud of the role I played in killing earmarks, which lots of members still complain to me about. Let them complain.) It was the era of Duke Cunningham and Bob Ney and Cassidy & Associates and Jack Abramoff and the PMA Group—all of the corruption that poured in when we as a party stopped being governed by principle and began instead to exist merely to win the next election.

When your raison d'être stops being *How can we hold to the principles of limited government and economic freedom?* and becomes *How can we hold on to this majority for one more cycle?* then you've become the very thing that you're supposed to be against. That corruption of the spirit opens the floodgates to actual corruption, and before long you have Congressman Cunningham giving his price list to lobbyists for "services rendered."

So we lost in 2006, and we deserved to lose.

But the Democrats learned from us too well, seeking only partisan advantage, governing without consensus. If you're not interested in a bipartisan majority for the policies that animate your governing philosophy, preferring instead to foment hatred for the other side, then you'll never have a chance to come to agreement and pass legislation that endures.

We have made this collapsed system work for no one but us. We used to play to a broader audience that demanded that we accomplish something. In this era of dysfunction and collapsed principle, our only accomplishment is painstakingly constructing the argument that we're not to blame and hoping that we've gerrymandered ourselves well enough to be safe in the next election. We decided that it was better to build and maintain a majority by using the levers of power rather than the art of persuasion and the battle of ideas. And we have decided that getting nothing done is okay. There are many on both sides who like this outcome so much that they think it's a good model on which to build a whole career. Far too often, we come to destroy, not to build.

As the country burns.

And our institutions are undermined.

And our values are compromised.

And the people become increasingly despondent and enraged.

And we become so estranged from our principles that we no longer recognize what principle is.

In my life, I have tried to conduct myself in a way that would make my parents proud and not embarrass my children. According to the dictates of my faith. I've always believed that politics will take care of itself, but principle—principle requires fidelity. And the older I get, the more that partisan pressure fades against the tenets of conscience.

It is not easy to oppose the presidential nominee of one's own party, and never in my life did I expect that circumstance to arise. My opposition to Donald Trump's candidacy did not escape his notice during the campaign, and we have had one memorable run-in. Just after he became the presumptive nominee of the Republican Party in the early summer of 2016, he came to a meeting of the Republican Caucus in the Senate.

"You've been very critical of me," Trump said, as I got up to introduce myself.

"Yes, I'm the other senator from Arizona—the one who didn't get captured—and I want to talk to you about statements

like that," I responded. I then asked him about immigration
and his comment about Mexicans being "rapists."

He brushed off the question and instead replied by saying
that I was going to lose my reelection. I had to inform him that
I wasn't on the fall ballot.

The papers played this encounter as: "GOP Senator Angrily
Confronts Trump at Closed Meeting."

For the record, I was not at all angry. I did want to talk about
what conservatives stand for beyond the smashmouth politics
that sometimes dominates campaigns. There was no such opportunity. But now is the time for a more serious conversation.

In 1960, Barry Goldwater, whose state I have the privilege to
represent in the United States Senate, published a book called
The Conscience of a Conservative. He wrote the book in response to what he saw as an emergency—the collapse of conservative principles, which in his view had been hopelessly
compromised by the New Deal. (Goldwater's book became one
of the most influential political books of all time, and it is seen
as the founding document of the modern conservative movement.) Today, I believe that conservatism has been compromised by something else. In the late 1990s, the conservative
gadfly Roger Stone began to observe, not disapprovingly, that
popular culture had become more influential than politics.
Stone was obviously onto something, for it now seems that conservatism has been compromised by a decidedly unconservative
stew of celebrity and authoritarianism. In these strange times,
it seems that a strong declaration of bedrock principle may well
constitute a radical act.

And in these strange times, I often think back to my first
years in Congress and contemplate why it is that any of us
serve.

I have a big family in Arizona, and once I got elected, everyone in my family became intensely curious about Washington.
To ensure that the weekends would not be taken up with having

to brief everyone separately, my wife, Cheryl, convinced me to start a tradition of writing a weekly update. An idealistic young conservative, I was possessed of the certainty that the solution to what ailed Washington had just walked into town. I had been in office scarcely a month when I wrote this:

Washington Update—February 3, 2001

It's Saturday afternoon, and I'm headed back to Washington from the Republican retreat at Williamsburg. These are giddy times for Republicans. To have control of both houses of Congress and the Presidency is something that hasn't happened since 1954. The sessions were productive, and it was great to get to know my colleagues better. I've developed a close friendship with several of the Freshman class, particularly Mike Pence. Prior to his arrival in Congress, Mike headed the Indiana Policy Review, a Think Tank in Fort Wayne. Mike shares my passion for marginal income tax rate cuts, and we played tag-team through much of the conference on the subject. Our goal is to ensure that the tax package being assembled leads with marginal rate cuts. Many of our colleagues would rather start by eliminating the marriage penalty and estate (death) tax. My feeling is that if we lead with these cuts, the Democrats will sign on, then refuse to go along with the more important parts of the package—marginal rate cuts.

In a meeting with Vice President Cheney, I brought up marginal rate cuts, and Mike Pence followed by urging the same, saying that he was part of the developing "Flake Caucus" that advocated rate cuts. Ric Keller, another Freshman, commented that we were starting to sound like the movie *Rain Man*, where the autistic lead character wanders around mumbling, in this case, "marginal rate tax cuts, definitely rate cuts."

We had a visit from President Bush while in Williamsburg. For the Freshmen, it was the second Friday lunch we had had with the President in a row. Last week we were invited to the White House, where we discussed his agenda with him. I had the chance to speak with the President, and encouraged him to stick to his plan to cut marginal rates. He responded emphatically "don't worry, don't worry!" So, things are looking good. I firmly believe that the best way to ensure that the economy stays strong is to cut taxes, and that the only way to limit the growth of government in the short term is to cut taxes.

It would seem that it would be easy for Republicans to do this. After all, Republicans were born to cut taxes. But it is not. What you learn fast around here is that the most important thing to nearly everyone here is to get reelected. Thus, taxes should only be cut if we can get credit for it and it will aid in reelection. It forces members of Congress to favor tax cuts like "correcting the marriage penalty," which plays better back in the district. Trouble is, correcting the marriage penalty wouldn't spur the economy and pales in comparison to marginal rate cuts in importance. . . .

My goodness. That young congressman was *obsessed* with tax cuts! In the early days, I pushed for every tax cut we could manage, especially marginal rates (at that time we were in a near-surplus situation), because I believe that lowering taxes usually begets more economic growth, which leads to higher tax revenue. There are limits to this model, of course. When Arthur Laffer sketched his curve on a napkin back in the 1970s, the highest tax rate was still 70 percent. Under those circumstances, bringing rates down to under 40 percent will obviously stimulate growth. Other types of tax cuts are far less stimulative, if they are stimulative at all. But those are good arguments to have.

During a 2012 Republican presidential debate, the candidates were asked if they would accept ten dollars in spending cuts for a one-dollar tax increase. None of them would take the deal. What were they thinking!? I would have *loved* that deal. The Simpson-Bowles plan to address our debt crisis called for 3-to-1 cuts to increases, and even that would likely have been better than any deal we could now strike.

I am not averse to revenue increases, as long as we cut entitlement spending by a larger amount. Otherwise, we have a structural deficit that will only get worse.

My point being: I am a conservative. We desperately need to get back to the rigorous and fact-based arguments that made us conservatives in the first place. But America is not just a collection of transactions, as some might have us believe. America is also a collection of vital ideas and precious values. And these are our values. These are our principles. They are our bedrock. They are not subject to change, owing to political fashion or cult of personality.

And that is why I am writing this book and taking this stand.

Let's draw back the curtain to establish how and why we have come to this. Let's reaffirm principle just as our principles are deeply in question. We must advance the cause of freedom by facing—as Senator Goldwater did in his time—the very real prospect that it could be taken from us.

This is not an act of apostasy. This is an act of fidelity.

CHAPTER TWO

QUESTIONING POWER

HIS HEART STOPPED.

And he would have died without the extraordinary skill of not one but two immigrants from majority-Muslim countries that had been compromised by terrorism.

A few days before the election, on November 3, my wife's father, Owen Bae, played two softball games, manning his usual position on the mound. But while he was reading the newspaper the next morning, a stabbing pain in his chest caused him to collapse onto the floor; he was barely able to tell his wife, Joyce, "I'm having a heart attack." An ambulance was called, and Owen was taken to Mercy Gilbert Medical Center in Gilbert, Arizona, where he had some preliminary tests done; in very critical condition, he was transferred to the Regional Medical Center in nearby Chandler, where an experienced cardiologist could tend to him.

That evening, a doctor named Fadi Khoury sat us down and informed us that Owen's aorta had ruptured. The rupture had somehow cauterized itself, temporarily at least, which is why Owen was still alive. However, Dr. Khoury explained, the mortality rate after such an event increased by 2 percent per hour, meaning that Owen would most likely not survive another forty-eight hours without surgery to repair the damage. My father-in-law was eighty-three, and surgery would be extremely risky. But it was the only hope.

A six-hour procedure was expected, but the lining of the aorta kept failing, so six hours turned into eleven hours, and after all of their efforts, Owen's heart wouldn't start. It simply refused to beat. The rupture had been too violent, the injury too grievous. Cheryl's father had survived the emergency, we thought, only to now die in intensive care. The bypass machine at Chandler Regional was not designed to keep a patient alive for much longer than eleven hours, so when Dr. Khoury emerged from the operating room to brief us, he said, "We'll give it one more shot in an hour," but added that if Owen's heart didn't start at that point, there was probably nothing else that could be done.

An hour later, his heart still wouldn't start, but Dr. Khoury had one last idea. That's when another doctor, this one named Jama Jahanyar, arrived from the Mayo Clinic in Scottsdale with a machine that would circulate and oxygenate Owen's blood and keep his body functioning for a longer period, giving his heart a better chance to recover. Even so, we had no idea if his heart would ever beat on its own again. But Dr. Jahanyar would not give up, leading a team of several doctors and nurses, performing several smaller surgeries over the ensuing two weeks to keep Owen alive as his heart healed.

Each of these doctors vested himself in Owen's care, and each refused to let him die without first exhausting himself and exhausting every last option to keep him alive. Both Dr. Khoury and Dr. Jahanyar have since visited Owen and Joyce, and they are now family to us. They each certainly could have thought, "He's lived a long life, this is where it should end." Instead they stayed up all night, postponed family trips, and fulfilled their obligations to a patient and his family in the most extraordinary way.

Fadi Khoury hadn't always been a brilliant cardiothoracic surgeon, of course. He had once been a Palestinian boy growing up amid unceasing violence and limited prospects. Jama Jahanyar had not always been a brilliant cardiothoracic surgeon, either. He was born in Afghanistan, a destroyed country similarly roiled by decades of war.

The stories of these two doctors are the stories of America— of striving, sometimes desperately, for a better life, of being willing to do anything and risk everything to get here. They are the stories of constant renewal brought by wave after wave of immigrants, creating our country over and over again, stories that have made America unique in the history of the world. Neither of these men started out life as "high-value migrants." Neither would likely have become who he became had he not made it to America. And neither might have been allowed into America had we restricted visas from countries compromised by terrorism.

That the executive orders were among the first acts of a new presidency sent a troubling signal to Americans of all backgrounds, as well as to the rest of the world, about what the next four years might bring. And while the Trump administration insisted that the president's executive orders suspending refugees from war-ravaged Syria indefinitely and restricting travel from seven (and then six) majority-Muslim countries was not a "Muslim ban," by early summer of 2017, several courts had ruled that a de facto Muslim ban is precisely what those orders sought to achieve.(By late June, the Supreme Court had allowed parts of the president's second order to go into effect pending a full review in the fall.) During the campaign, candidate Trump had made no pretense to doing anything else. In America, we do not favor one religion over another, and we do not believe in guilt by association, no matter what any man might think of any given religion, or what problems some adherents of any faith might be causing in the name of that religion.

In fact, in December 2015, after candidate Trump called for a ban on all Muslims from entering the United States, I found the act to be so morally repugnant and un-American that I issued a statement on Twitter: "Just when you think @realDonaldTrump can stoop no lower, he does. These views do not reflect serious thought." Then my family and I attended afternoon prayers at the Islamic Center of the North East Valley, in Scottsdale, to let the congregation know that most Americans were not given to such intolerance. "I'll bet you never thought you would see a Mormon speaking in a mosque," I began my talk. "I think this is a surprise for me, too. We all know how we are different, but let me tell you a few ways that we are similar. . . ."

The next day, I received a note from George W. Bush, who as president led the country through the grave and mournful period after September 11, 2001. He also had visited a mosque to offer important reassurance and to make the crucial and obvious distinction between Muslims and radical jihadis:

Dear Jeff,
    I saw your speech to the mosque in your state. I was deeply moved by your remarks. Moved by your leadership, your thoughtful tone, your reminder of the importance of religious freedom and your warm humor. Thank you for your voice of reason in these unreasonable times. . . .

During the campaign, I assumed that this shocking episode—among so many more—would be a political blunder from which Donald Trump would not recover. I readily concede that I got the politics wrong. I will even concede that I underestimated the populist appeal of Trump's proposed Muslim ban. But I will not concede the underlying principle of religious freedom. If principle is only defended when there's nothing at stake, then it is probably not much of a principle after all.

Moreover, in the case of global jihad, we are provoking civilizational struggle between Islam and the West, or as historian Niall Ferguson has put it, between "the West and the rest." Banning Muslims from America, or even appearing to do so, apart from being unconstitutional, would give the jihadis precisely the struggle they want, with the vast and varied Islamic world caught in between, some small percentage of them vulnerable to a radicalization that we could plausibly bear some responsibility for. In fact, when word of the president's first executive order spread on the Internet shortly after ink met paper at the Pentagon on January 27, dark jihadi cul-de-sacs online filled with praise for President Trump's "blessed ban." And so the legitimate targets of the president's policy found perverse pleasure in the order.

I find it difficult to believe that this could possibly have been the president's intention. In fact, as for President Trump's executive actions themselves, I believe he is in earnest when he says that he wants to do everything in his power to defend America, her allies, and her interests—however much he may distort the dangers and manipulate the understandable fears of Americans.

Moreover, in the matter of both executive orders singling out the list of majority-Muslim countries, I believe that the president was probably on solid constitutional ground in issuing the orders. Under the Constitution, the president is granted broad authority to enforce borders and protect citizens inside those borders. But there is a world of difference between believing that you *can* do something and that you *should* do something. I believe that the president's decision to bar entry from certain majority-Muslim countries is profoundly misguided—both because it runs counter to American values and because it makes no strategic sense. In fact, it could end up producing the opposite strategic effect than is intended—making us less, not more, secure.

That's where the wisdom of deliberation comes in. It is that deliberation that is one of the principal features of American conservatism as a coherent governing philosophy. If conservatives do not believe in the calm, sober use and restraint of government power, then we believe in nothing. Especially when it is exercised in haste, arbitrarily, and without deliberation or care. There is the *trust your gut, shoot from the hip* approach to political decision-making, and then there is the *fly off the handle* approach. As evidenced by the 2016 presidential campaign, flying off the handle is a big, big hit right now—at least in terms of its entertainment value and ratings.

In this book I mean to establish that as a governing philosophy, the instability of flying off the handle is a disaster for the United States and is profoundly unconservative. The same goes for our state-of-the-art presidential bellicosity—which seems to be quite popular in "conservative" circles these days. That is the antithesis of conservatism, too. And it is also very often the antithesis of truth.

The White House's list of forbidden countries was mysteriously selective, barring people from these shores without regard to whether their countries of origin actually have a history of exporting terrorism to America—in fact, the list left out the countries that have produced the most terrorism we've seen perpetrated here. So if countering terrorism is the goal, the policy doesn't make sense on its face. But when the president's executive order came under legal challenge and public scrutiny, the White House responded by saying that the seven countries covered by the president's order had in fact been designated as "countries of concern" by President Obama and intimated that in designating those countries in his orders, President Trump was somehow merely continuing the counterterrorism work of his predecessor. Well, I knew better.

After the ISIS attack on Paris in November 2015, in which 130 people were killed and hundreds more were wounded, there was intense pressure brought to bear here in the United States to stop the flow of refugees, from Syria in particular and from Iraq as well. Now, we have not taken in many Syrian refugees to date—most of our smaller allies have taken in many more—and some of us on Capitol Hill thought that it was a mistake and unfair to blame refugees and exaggerate the risk they pose, as they are already subjected to a rigorous vetting process that can take years to complete.

Of greater immediate concern were Frenchmen and Belgians, for instance, who travel to Syria or Iraq to fight with ISIS, return to their home country, and then—because of our visa-waiver agreement with most of Europe and a few other countries—are free to board a flight to come to the United States, with no visa and no questions asked.

I love the visa-waiver arrangement. Most of us do, as it is reciprocal and allows for easy, visa-free travel to and from thirty-eight countries for American citizens. But there were very real vulnerabilities when it came to possible European jihadis seeking to travel to the United States under the radar, exploiting this practice of practical convenience to potentially do harm. (This, thankfully, had not to that point been a problem.) So in the spring of 2016, not long after the Paris attacks, Democratic senator Dianne Feinstein and I introduced an amendment prohibiting anyone from the visa-waiver countries who had recently traveled to Iraq or Syria from taking advantage of the visa-waiver program. In other words, they would first need to be interviewed, in order to discover the circumstances of their travel. Simple—or so I thought.

Suddenly, what started as a focused effort to close that one loophole morphed into a broader waiver exclusion policy. In the House of Representatives, the House Judiciary Committee took up the issue, and countries began to be rather arbitrarily added to the list. Now, instead of just the spots of current conflict, countries from which we could document a risk, other countries were added—Libya, Somalia, Sudan, Yemen. Sudan, which *is* a source and sponsor of terrorism, doesn't enjoy the visa-waiver program under any circumstances anyway, so adding it to the list made no sense. There seemed to be some other agenda at work. For good measure, the House negotiators added Iran, of course, and this addition has proven to have a very negative and unjustified effect on many Iranian American friends in Arizona and around the country who have had their travel curbed for no apparent reason.

It is difficult to find successful tech firms in Silicon Valley that don't have Iranian Americans in positions of leadership. Groups like Persian Tech Entrepreneurs and others are a testament to their growing talent and influence. But it's not just Silicon Valley—by any metric, Iranians in America, many of them having fled Khomeini's revolution, have become successful, and become American. Those of Iranian descent born in Europe or the United States have often had dual citizenship automatically conferred on them by Tehran, often without their knowledge. When you impose a travel ban involving Iran, you're going to affect a lot of people traveling to do business and to visit family.

As for the visa-waiver issue, it's worth keeping in mind that when we stop allowing Europeans in automatically, European visa-waiver countries might reciprocate, which burdens Americans a lot more than it does the Europeans, because all of a sudden there are thirty-eight countries that Americans have to get a visa to travel to. The common-sense fix that Senator Feinstein and I had hoped to achieve was, in the face of the broader House list, becoming a mess. But the Obama administration was so fearful that the Congress was on the path to doing away with the refugee program altogether that it swallowed the expanded list. Senators Durbin, Heller, Feinstein, and I pressed the White House not to concede to the expanded list—that doing so would create all sorts of unintended and unnecessary problems—and we also lobbied House Judiciary Committee chairman Bob Goodlatte and Speaker of the House Paul Ryan to limit our visa-waiver amendment to just Syria and Iraq, but by then the cake was baked.

And that's how we got that list.

But under questions and pressure, in the atmosphere of a new administration, all of a sudden the list of forbidden countries became "Obama's list," with all sorts of rigor being ascribed to its formulation, as if it had been carried down the mountain on stone tablets rather than being haphazardly assembled as it was bounced around House committees.

I was puzzled when the new president's senior advisor Stephen Miller—who was also credited with a principal role in the development of the travel ban—appeared on national television and announced that "our opponents, the media, and the whole world will soon see as we begin to take further actions, that the powers of the president to protect our country are very substantial and *will not be questioned.*" Will not be questioned? *Really?*

Presidential power should be questioned, continually. That's what our system of government, defined by the separation of powers, is all about. It shouldn't matter whether the president belongs to my party or to another one.

Besides, I'm from the west. Questioning power is what we do.

CHAPTER THREE

ON BAD INFORMATION AND THE THREAT TO DEMOCRACY

"To see what is in front of one's nose needs a constant struggle," George Orwell wrote. "One thing that helps toward it is to keep a diary, or, at any rate, to keep some kind of record of one's opinions about important events. Otherwise, when some particularly absurd belief is exploded by events, one may simply forget that one ever held it."

When one is in the business of government, one is, with discouraging regularity, in the business of absurd beliefs. And governments and political parties using false or misleading information to press an advantage or advance policy goals—or occasionally just to deceive and manipulate the public—is nothing new. But so frenzied is this new age of absurd beliefs, so fast and furious do they fly at us from every direction, we would do well to heed Orwell's admonition to remember just how far off the deep end we sometimes allow ourselves to go. If we forget, it all begins to seem normal.

After all, it is Orwell who gave his name to a term that is meant as a bulwark against normalizing the patently abnormal:

Orwellian, a word that seems quaint now, inadequate to our moment. Lucky for Orwell that he never made it to Washington to see what goes on. In this new age, we will have to think up new words to describe the previously indescribable.

However much President Trump may have had the constitutional authority to initiate a travel ban or to shut down the flow of refugees to the United States, the policy as conceived by the White House was predicated on a meaningless list. On bad information. To be clear, in the context of the burgeoning phenomenon that has come to be known as "fake news," the president's travel ban list was a fairly minor offense. And it at least was rooted in a discussion of serious policy. The same cannot be said for many other vexing presidential statements, the purpose of which is harder to figure.

Whatever the source, a steady diet of bad information, conveyed in bad faith, can over time become a serious threat to a democracy. Over time, a determined effort to undermine the very idea of truth softens the ground for anti-democratic impulses. This is why the Founders felt it critical that an American electorate be well informed, and why being a discerning and informed citizen is now more important than ever before.

Fake news has been around forever. Our own time, of course, has put its distinctive mark on this scourge. We haven't, for instance, always had the technology to disseminate and target fake news in such a way that millions of people believe it to be true, the way we do now. We haven't always had to deal with weaponized information as a means to wage war by foreign enemy powers. We haven't always had the willingness and brazenness of certain politicians to exploit the gullibility of certain voters by pushing fake news. Perhaps most destructive of all, we haven't ever had an occupant of the White House who so routinely calls true reports that irk him "fake news" while giving his seal of approval to fake reports that happen to support his position. This is tremendously damaging; the words of a president are more resonant than those of any other leader on earth, and it is difficult to unlearn false things once learned. The reasonable and patriotic impulse is to want to believe what the president says. I certainly want to believe, as do the people of my state.

But it is madness to turn ourselves inside out in an attempt to make reality comport with an alternate reality, just because someone in power would like us to. And whether the embrace of "alternative facts" at the highest levels of American life is intended as some sort of political strategy or as a principle of cacophony, either way it creates a state of confusion, dividing us along fissures of truth and falsity and keeping us in a kind of low-level dread, continually off-balance in a way that government should not do—and certainly never on purpose.

Near the beginning of the document that made us free, our Declaration of Independence, Jefferson writes: "We hold these truths to be self-evident. . . ." From the beginning, our freedom has been predicated on truth. Enduring democracies depend on the acceptance of shared facts, facts such as: certified elections are valid, millions of votes were not illegally cast in the 2016 election, vaccinations don't cause autism, and two Hawaiian newspapers announcing the birth of Barack Obama more than fifty years ago probably means that Obama was born in Hawaii—just to highlight a few of the more colorful examples of the nonsense that has made the rounds in recent years.

Too little in American life is "self-evident" now. And of course, what those aforementioned facts have in common is the president, who is or has been an enthusiastic purveyor of each at various times. This penchant for false reports and conspiracy theories is not something that we can take lightly or dismiss as "just politics." And it is not something that we can embrace or tolerate if we want to be a heathy political movement or expect anyone to take us seriously.

Only in anti-democratic propaganda states do we see "alternate facts" successfully compete with the truth for primacy. Only in such states do we see a sustained program of bad information emanate from the highest levels of the government. This, as I will continue to point out in the course of this book, is not a conservative value. And as conservatives, we simply cannot carry on as if it is not happening.

Our current crisis with the truth itself can probably be traced back to the aforementioned "birther" controversy. The theory that Barack Obama had not been born in the United States and thus was not a legitimate president took hold with a vengeance in my state; in early 2011, the Arizona State Legislature was consumed with the question. Legislation was introduced requiring presidential candidates to provide a valid birth certificate to Arizona's secretary of state in order to appear on Arizona's ballot. That legislation ultimately passed before being vetoed by Arizona governor Jan Brewer.

Skepticism about the president's birthplace was stoked by the sheriff of Maricopa County, Joe Arpaio, who would ultimately send investigators to Hawaii to examine the president's birth certificate and question critics of the president, who, not surprisingly, more than fifty years after the fact, could not recall the birth. (Sheriff Arpaio, after losing his sixth reelection bid in November 2016, convened his final press conference a month later to announce that after a five-year investigation, he had concluded that the President's birth certificate had indeed been forged.)

On February 17, 2011, three days after I announced my campaign for the Senate, I was interviewed on CNN on the topic of the president's birthplace. I said that Republicans needed to "get off this kick" and accept reality, that if we oppose President Obama, it should not be based on questions of his legitimacy, but because our ideas for America were better than his. This was not received well by some of the conservative base in Arizona, who felt that I was "taking sides" with the president. I preferred to think of it as being on the side of empirical truth.

During this period I spoke at the Red Mountain Tea Party, one of the larger and better-organized Tea Party groups around the valley. This group met every month with several hundred in attendance. I fully expected to receive the "Do you believe the president is a citizen?" question, and sure enough, when the question came, I said that if we wanted to be taken seriously, we had to stop indulging in ugly conspiracy theories. Those words were met with a chorus of boos.

When a conspiracy theory becomes litmus-test orthodoxy, objective reality is at risk.

I am very supportive of conservative media, was weaned on William F. Buckley Jr.'s magazine *National Review* and TV show *Firing Line,* and I believe that any honest critique of the American media landscape over the past fifty years or so must acknowledge that the press has generally been more favorably inclined to liberals over conservatives. But the truth is the truth, and anything else is a waste of time. Still, to be booed because I didn't subscribe to a right-wing conspiracist fantasy about our first African American president is a sobering experience indeed. The impact of the support the absurd birther theory regularly received on certain shows on Fox News cannot be overstated. In fact, the impact of the conditioning that the minds of American conservatives receive on some of these Fox shows also cannot be overstated. The same of course goes for some of the programming at MSNBC and any other outlet whose obligation isn't so much to the truth as it is to confecting a daily narrative that is agreeable to its selected audience. Sometimes, for our own good, we should all just change the channel.

Four years after that Tea Party meeting, traveling on Air Force One with President Obama on a flight to Kenya as the lone Republican in a congressional delegation of nineteen, I wondered how many of my fellow Arizonans still believed that we were traveling to the land of the president's birth.

In the 2016 election, I did not support Hillary Clinton for president. My opposition to her candidacy was due to the profound policy disagreements I had with her. My opposition wasn't rooted in a belief that she was evil. But to survey the "conservative" information landscape during the summer and fall before the election, you would have thought that she was not only unsuited for the presidency but also that she was indeed one of the darkest figures in human history—guilty of all manner of heinous atrocities. And by atrocities, I mean nothing rooted in her service as secretary of state, including the tragic loss of life at the American diplomatic mission in Benghazi, Libya, which is a completely valid area of inquiry, rooted in real events. Rather, I mean atrocities of such vivid and sordid detail that they could have been invented only in the most feverish chat rooms of the most conspiratorial websites on the Internet.

For years, elements of the right wing—including members of Congress—have trafficked in lists of people that Bill and Hillary Clinton have supposedly had murdered. And in a more recent example of outrageous alternate reality, by the election of 2016 the right-wing Internet was ablaze with stories of how the former secretary of state and Democratic nominee for president was the supposed leader of a massive international child-enslavement ring run out of a pizza parlor in Washington, D.C., and of how her campaign chairman, John Podesta, also said to be part of this ring, engaged in satanic rituals as well. The origin of this story seems to have been a white supremacist Twitter account, from which it was then amplified, as are so many of these deranged fantasies, in the comments sections of 4chan and Reddit before virally making its way to more mainstream outlets and becoming a story of truly global proportions.

Never mind that there were more than enough serious and legitimate reasons to oppose and defeat Hillary Clinton. So many people on my side were too eager to reach for and spread conspiracy theories, too eager to believe in premises that were demonstrably false—among them senior aides to our presidential candidate. This impulse to dehumanize, to ascribe the worst possible motives to people who in more normal times would be regarded not as "the enemy" but merely as political opponents, is a signal that something is terribly wrong. It's a symptom of a serious disease in the body politic—which my Senate colleague from Nebraska, Ben Sasse, has described as "a civilization-warping crisis of public trust" and which, left untreated, could be fatal to our democratic system of government.

Some liberals so hated George W. Bush that they felt compelled to invent fictional grievances to harbor against him— a political phenomenon that came to be known in some circles as "Bush Derangement Syndrome." Some conservatives compounded this unfortunate trend during the presidency of Barack Obama, inventing a Manchurian straw-man president whose motives were so thoroughly evil that for the good of the country, the thinking went, he simply *had* to be vanquished. Responsible conservatives face the conditions of the world as they are and don't go tilting at phantoms. And we certainly don't encourage that kind of behavior in others.

There is a particularly obnoxious email that periodically finds its way into my inbox, detailing the luxurious lifestyle led by members of Congress. It is usually greeted with a "not this again" shrug from my wife, Cheryl, as she cuts my hair. Among other lavish perks, according to the email's author, once they are elected, members of the House and Senate receive their full congressional salaries for life. No matter how many times the information is debunked by Snopes and other reputable news outlets, the false information fights its way back into the mainstream because many people *want* to believe that it is true.

But what is there to be done, when the technology has so radically changed the pace of life itself and lends itself so easily to deception on a mass scale? Far too often the Internet is where the truth goes to die. And it is those precincts of the Internet that have given rise to so many of the false reports and conspiracy theories that fuel some contemporary conservative thought and much conservative rage and that threaten to create an alternate conservative reality altogether, with the shared facts and consensus-building necessary for the survival of democracy left in severe peril.

Let me be clear: "Fake news" is a problem that knows no party. Bad information is and has been propagated by all sides and by profiteers (paid trolls and bot farms in the Balkans, among many other places) who have no ideology at all, other than mayhem. But as a conservative, it is my own side and its role in the deterioration of facts and truth—and its eager susceptibility to propaganda—that I will concern myself with here.

We are only as good as our information, and if we lose our sense of objective truth, we lose everything. We must protect and preserve our healthy public sphere—that civic space in which we vigorously debate and negotiate, agree and disagree—or else.

The information ecosystem as it exists online has enabled the creation of alternative truths, which wear down our ability to discern truth from falsity and could, with time, hobble our capacity to care. And that is an existential threat to America, just as sure as North Korea or a nuclear-armed Iran are existential threats. Perhaps even more so, because we are doing this to ourselves.

As conservatives, it is essential that we defend our prerogatives and positions not just against bad information from the left but against bad information from the right as well. We can and must criticize different sources of information, different journalistic outfits, different networks, different newspapers, different magazines, different websites, and different parts of the culture when they get the facts wrong. But if we are to have continued legitimacy, we must also be willing to criticize ourselves. There was once a time in politics, as well as in journalism, when in order to be serious and credible, you had to observe a baseline fidelity to empirical truth. And if you made mistakes—or worse, if you were a bad actor and got things wrong on purpose—you suffered real consequences. Violate the public trust, and you paid a steep price. The higher up the food chain you went, the more serious and credible you were expected to be.

That order seems to have vanished.

Today, wrong answers and crackpot theories compete for attention online, on an equal footing with good information. Once, bad information was self-marginalizing in the marketplace of ideas, and reality-based information—those "shared facts" I referred to earlier—was front and center in the civic space where we strenuously argued over policy. Today, CNN and *The New York Times* are called fake news by some people on our side, while the president personally thanks infowars. com and its founder Alex Jones for "standing up for the values that makes this country great." Jones, it must be noted, has rarely met a bizarre conspiracy that he didn't fully embrace and is one of the most egregious polluters of civil discourse in America. He believes, for instance, that 9/11 was perpetrated by the American government and that the massacre at Sandy Hook Elementary School in December 2012, in which twenty firstgraders were killed, was a hoax staged by the government as a pretext to confiscate our guns. Those grieving parents that we all saw were—according to Jones—paid actors. It was disheartening to learn that in the days immediately following his election, as President-Elect Trump was receiving the well wishes of world leaders, he also took time to place a call to this man to let him know how important his support had been to the success of his campaign.

Giving away one's agency and becoming captive to such outlandish and vile alternative facts would be bad enough were one an average person, quietly living his or her life. But giving away one's agency to such a confusion of fact and fantasy when one has power—well, that is truly dangerous. And it is something else, too: highly influential. Bad information propagated by powerful people spreads like a contagion, infecting vulnerable people in its path.

Some of our Western allies are so concerned about the threat posed by fake news that they are considering imposing enormous civil penalties on the social networks that spread it and profit from it. Some proposals even criminalize the content itself. In the months after our election, as worries of Russian meddling and an awareness of the magnitude of the problem crossed the Atlantic to threaten parliamentary elections in Germany and France, the German minister of the interior proposed to fine Facebook and Twitter $53 million for each instance of fake news that is not removed from circulation within twenty-four hours.

That is an extreme position. In the United States, we have the First Amendment, and so a solution to the scourge of fake news that involves the silencing power of the government is both abhorrent and out of the question. In my view, a government "solution" like this often serves only to compound the problem. And in the instance of global information businesses that have in the range of two billion customers connected by a common technology, policy makers in Washington are simply not nimble enough to do anything but blunder in with their good intentions and make things worse.

But that doesn't absolve us of the responsibility of defending truth as if our democracy depends on it. Because it does. And something must be done about those who would wage an

information war against us—from both without and within—
and against our institutions and our democratic norms. Yes,
fake news has been around forever, but the means by which to
disseminate it on a massive scale have gone from paltry to
global in just a few years. Seldom if ever in human history have
we witnessed such an explosive social experiment, and seldom
have we had less understanding of the effect of technology on
us, both as a society and as individuals, and seldom have we
seen businesses with the potential to do both good and harm
grow with such speed and on such a grand scale. Countermea-
sures from the Pentagon and our national security apparatus to
combat this problem notwithstanding, this is where market solutions come in. Simply put: Bad information has to become
bad for business.

Even the technologists and the social media goliaths are
having to race to stay clear about what it is they're selling and
about what is and isn't true. In the early months of 2017, CBS's
60 Minutes devoted a segment to the subject of fake news,
where it reported that in Michigan (for example) in the days
before the election, fully half of the information in circulation
on social media was fraudulent. And during its investigation
into Russian meddling into our 2016 election, the Senate Intelligence Committee interviewed a former FBI agent named Clinton Watts, who revealed that the Russians, who are now
wielding fake news as a weapon of war, had during the election
used "trolls" to expertly plant false stories in the American
news ecosystem, stories that were amplified geometrically by
Russian "bots," machine-run Twitter accounts that share stories artificially, causing them to go viral. To most consumers of
social media, it is impossible to tell if a story is popular because
a lot of actual humans have read and shared it or because bots
have gamed the system. And of course, "likes" and "shares"
give the illusion of credibility and are also the basis for the social media business models. Watts's testimony before the Senate

was particularly chilling. "Until we get a firm basis on fact and fiction in our own country," he said, "get some agreement about the facts, whether it be 'Do I support the intelligence community or do I instead believe a story I read on my Twitter feed?' we're going to have a big problem."

And when 600 million people (and counting) see a news story every week on Facebook, the impact of that platform is profound. No news organization in the world can claim anything close to that kind of reach. So those stories had better be right. Ironically, it was a highly contested claim that turned Facebook on its head in advance of the 2016 election and led to a dramatic proliferation of websites peddling false reports.

In the spring of 2016, complaints that Facebook was suppressing conservative news started appearing in conservative comments sections on the web (comments sections of all stripes seem to be a common breeding ground for fake news) before popping up on other websites. At issue was the "Trending Topics" feature of Facebook, which is supposed to be based on the volume of interest a given subject is achieving at a given time and determines how many people on Facebook will be exposed to the subject. A report on the tech website Gizmodo quoted a former Facebook "news curator" who said that conservative viewpoints were sometimes "black-listed," which, if true, was a very disturbing allegation.

Facebook founder Mark Zuckerberg denied the claim but, recognizing the seriousness of the issue, convened a round-table in May 2016 with conservative media figures, including Glenn Beck, S. E. Cupp, Dana Perino, and Brent Bozell (Breitbart.com, then still run by Steve Bannon, was invited but declined to attend) to give assurances and seek solutions. Zuckerberg released a statement, which read in part: "To serve our diverse community, we are committed to building a platform for all ideas. Trending Topics is designed to surface the most newsworthy and popular conversations on Facebook. We have rigorous guidelines that do not permit the prioritization of one viewpoint over another or the suppression of political perspectives."

Three months later, Zuckerberg did something unexpected: He fired Facebook's entire Trending Topics staff of eighteen human editors and turned the function over entirely to algorithms. Making the decisions agnostic—based not on biases but on data—appeared to solve the problem. Owing to the law of unintended consequences, however, the decision did more than level the playing field—it turned the playing field upside down and inside out. As flawed as the news curators may have been, an essential part of their job was determining the factual accuracy of trending topics and bringing a story's real-world validity to bear on the decision of whether to include it in Trending Topics or not.

With the humans gone, the bots took over. And the fake news sites grew exponentially overnight.

After the election, a study by Buzzfeed reported that "hyperpartisan political Facebook pages and websites are consistently feeding their millions of followers false or misleading information," with one of the worst offenders being a group of pro-Trump websites originating in Macedonia, which played a "significant role in propagating" false pro-Trump articles. A seventeen-year-old Macedonian boy contacted by Buzzfeed said, "I started the site for an easy way to make money."

And it's not just the low-information and propaganda-fed among us who are susceptible to the seventeen-year-old Macedonians, either. In a world that has changed as quickly as ours has, the reliability of information has become a matter of our national security, and we are all vulnerable. The problem is infinitely compounded when the political class not only doesn't reject this nonsense but also embraces it as a useful tactic.

There is a saying many of us grew up hearing: "Garbage in, garbage out." Defending our political prerogatives by filling our heads with propaganda is not a virtue, and it certainly cannot be called conservative. As conservatives, we believe in the marketplace. If we aren't confident enough to take our ideas to the people and confident enough that they'll be heard, especially given the political hegemony we currently enjoy, then I am not sure that we deserve that hegemony. A reliance on mis- or disinformation betrays a lack of confidence in our defining ideas, a lack of commitment to our core principles, and it contributes to the decline of the country we love. I have said it before, and I'll say it again: We must get off this kick.

CHAPTER FOUR

CONSCIENCE OF A CONSERVATIVE

A COUPLE OF MONTHS into the Trump administration, as word of factional tension began to spill out of the White House—between the hard-right advisors who had helped elect the president on one side and members of the president's family on the other—Michael Gerson, the conservative writer and former senior aide to President George W. Bush, wrote in *The Washington Post*:

> This inbuilt discord has turned normal West Wing tension into a red-carpeted cage fight. A Republican with recent White House interaction told me: "Watching them work was frankly terrifying. They fear each other, they hate each other, they are paranoid beyond belief and it doesn't work."
>
> And it should concern conservatives that neither side in the main White House conflict—ethno-nationalists or moderates related to the president—is actually conservative. It would be better for the Republican Party (and for

the world) if the family were to win this contest, as it almost certainly will.

That change would make the administration marginally more humane. *But it would not, for the most part, be a victory for conservative policy ideas.*

Emphasis mine.

As long as there has been politics, there has been internecine bloodletting. But we have never seen anything quite like this before. And at its root is a vacancy of conviction and core beliefs. This is what happens when we exalt tactical victories over principle, give in to the politics of expediency and resentment, and forget who we are and what we are supposed to stand for.

So what do we even mean when we talk about conservatism? Let me tell you something of my conservatism and where it came from.

It is the honor of my life to hold one of the two seats in the United States Senate from Arizona. It has also been my honor to follow in the tradition of another Arizona conservative—and the founder of what we think of as the modern conservative movement—Barry Goldwater. In a quirk of history, both my fellow senator John McCain and I can claim to hold Goldwater's seat in the Senate, as Goldwater held both of Arizona's seats at different times—the seat I hold before he ran for president in 1964, and the seat Senator McCain holds afterward. Senator McCain might agree that Senator Goldwater has left some mighty big shoes to fill.

I often wonder what Barry Goldwater would make of the current state of his party and of American politics more generally. I am confident that he would not be pleased or amused.

In 1960, Senator Goldwater declared his conservative principles in the classic book that lends this modest work its name. In Goldwater's spare assessment, *The Conscience of a Conservative* was a clarion call to a country that had lost its way in a morass of federal bureaucracy, and a manifesto to reclaim our founding values before it was too late. It was a document that saw malign intent in centralized power, and the emergency to which Goldwater's treatise represented a response was the bloated statism brought on by the excesses of Franklin Roosevelt's New Deal. There are specific powers granted to the government under the Constitution, and Goldwater was hard-pressed to find much of the modern welfare state in those enumerated powers. But the movement of men and nations financed by the central government can take on a Newtonian momentum all its own; it begins to seem inexorable. In Goldwater's reckoning, when the government intersects with the life of a man, the result—even if there may be some temporary benefit—is almost never good. To him, the modern struggle was between an independent and enlightened conservatism and a stagnant repression that robbed individuals of dignity and independence. If the situation wasn't reversed, the powers absorbed by the state would, as the country grew, usurp the innate freedoms of the people in such a way that those freedoms would be impossible to recover—with the people forever robbed of dignity and the character of the country itself forever changed.

The world that received Goldwater's book was a world of creeping government power, on both sides of the Iron Curtain. Our great civilizational struggle with global communism was at the time still an open question, feverishly engaged: Which system best met the needs of mankind? Did democracy matter? Was freedom that important? In Goldwater's view, it was difficult to make the best case for free markets and liberal Western democracy when our own government had such a claim on our lives that the top tax rate was 91 percent, when there was a lifetime claim to welfare benefits, and when our "free markets"—highly and increasingly regulated—were anything but free.

Goldwater's crisis was that the Republican Party had been rendered a poor vehicle for conservative values due to sustained proximity to wildly successful New Dealers and had been corrupted by them. This exposure to Rooseveltism had turned Republicans into soft or phony conservatives, or worse still: They mistakenly thought that what they were doing *was* conservatism.

As a man of the west, Goldwater wanted absolutely nothing to do with the New Deal or what came after. Also as a man of the west, he didn't mind fighting battles all alone, against overwhelming prevailing sentiment. He was stubborn that way.

Born in the Arizona Territory in the first decade of the twentieth century, three years before statehood, Goldwater, inasmuch as he was aware of government at all growing up, had only reason to be wary of it. Whether it was water rights, or land use, or the federal government laying physical claim to half of his new state, Goldwater had no use for Washington, D.C. Whereas New Dealers saw the Tenth Amendment as the Founding Fathers' afterthought, the western man saw in Madison's beautifully crafted twenty-eight words the centerpiece of the United States Constitution, establishing strict constraints on government authority and affirming the autonomy of the people: "The powers not delegated to the United States by the Constitution, nor prohibited by it to the States, are reserved to the States respectively, or to the people."

Goldwater's translation: Buzz off, federal government. We'll call if we need you. Don't hold your breath.

I was born in the state that Goldwater made, in a town smaller than the Phoenix of Goldwater's childhood. There are no halls of power in Snowflake, Arizona, population 5,590. There is no need for such trappings and affectations when you've got the Mogollon Rim, the southern edge of the Colorado Plateau that you have to climb up and over to reach my little town from Phoenix. It is surely a test for the most dedicated travelers, but the Rim Country rewards you with the most spectacular view—in the state that has the most spectacular views in all the world.

The Flakes weren't always so enchanted by the Arizona

landscape, though. We became Arizonans in 1878, when Brigham Young himself had sent my great-great-grandfather, William Jordan Flake, and others down from Utah to colonize the area. Legend has it that after experiencing Arizona's rugged and unforgiving terrain, some colonizers returned to Utah and told Brigham Young that there was nothing worth settling down there.

But Brigham Young had instructed William Jordan to sell everything that he owned—including all of his land holdings in rich Utah bottomland. His exact words were, "Leave nothing to come back to." And so he did, and he eventually would purchase the valley where Snowflake is today. Shortly thereafter he met up with Erastus Snow, the Mormon apostle who was overseeing the church's colonization efforts, and they combined their names to give my town its name.

My great-great-grandfather was a rancher, and he passed some of the land down to his son, James Madison Flake, and James Madison passed some of it down to my grandfather Virgil Maeser, who passed it down to four of his sons, the eldest of whom is my father, Dean Flake. And that land—the F-Bar Ranch—is where I grew up.

When I go home today, I get to appreciate the view, but when you're a kid on a cattle ranch, you work. I drove the windrower untold miles over our alfalfa fields and baled thousands of bales of hay. The windrower has a fourteen-foot blade, and when I was five years old, I put my right index finger where it wasn't supposed to be and lost a half-inch or so of it off the top. My dad wrapped my bloody hand tightly in his handkerchief, put me up in the truck, and finished the job before taking me to the only doctor in town to get it seen to. The missing piece was reattached, only to fall off three weeks later as I swam in the community pool. "Mom!" I hollered. "My finger fell off!" My mother, ever dignified and measured, brought her intact index finger to her lips with admirable discretion. *"Shhhhhhhh,"* she admonished. She didn't want me to scare anybody. Such was life with eleven kids. The battle scar didn't keep me from doing my chores (by that point, my dad had lost *three* fingers to ranch life), and as I got older, in the pre-dawn, on days when my father was shorthanded, he'd come into the room I shared with five of my brothers and say, "Who wants to ride today?" If we were willing to work, there'd be no school that day. All of my teachers knew that when it was time to round up and brand calves, my main purpose in life was to be ranch hand for my dad and the brothers of the F-Bar. And the initiation for new girlfriends was always taking them out to witness the pregnancy testing of cows or the castration of bulls. (Trust me when I say that that was a test of true love.)

From a very young age in ranch country, you also get to know immigrants intimately and honestly. You learn through experience how indispensable they are to making things work in America. It seems that once every generation or so, we have these spasms of immigrant resentment and scapegoating, if not outright hatred. We are at our worst when we give in to these impulses and resort to a device that can be emotionally satisfying, perhaps, and politically expedient but very self-destructive—the impulse to look for somebody else to blame for our problems. *If only these people weren't here, we would be much better off.* The nativist impulse is always destructive, always comes with a cost, and never ends well.

I've had a lifetime of direct experience with immigration. I would say that every farm of any size in the country has. On the ranch, we employed migrant labor for jobs large and small—moving sprinkler pipes, driving farm equipment, baling hay, building fence, and taking care of essential maintenance tasks. In the 1970s and early 1980s, as testimony to the incoherence of our intentions and political imperatives, it wasn't illegal to hire them but it *was* illegal for them to be here. There was virtually no Border Patrol on the border itself, and migrants could come and go with relative ease. But periodically, the Border Patrol would come up to farms like ours in northern Arizona, conduct raids, and take migrant workers back. Our mechanic Manuel was taken back to Mexico by the Border Patrol nineteen times. And sometimes when the end of the season came and the workers needed a ride back home, they would simply find a Border Patrol agent and get themselves picked up. My life was made far more difficult during the middle of summer when the Border Patrol would raid our farm. Sometimes the Border Patrol would send small planes to search our alfalfa fields for migrants. When I would hear the distinctive whine of the Cessna, I'd hop on a horse, put on a hat that would obscure my head, and try to divert the Border Patrol away from our workers—a decoy in the game of cat and mouse.

When crossing the border could be done frequently and easily, the workers didn't tend to bring their families, because they did not intend to stay. And so there was a much healthier circular pattern of migration than we have today. It was when we really started to clamp down on the border and make it difficult and expensive to cross—so that crossing involved hiring "coyotes"—that once-seasonal workers would bring their families with them and stay in the United States. Given those circumstances, it just made sense for them to do so.

Of course, cartel activity near the border and criminal aliens are very real concerns, and such activity necessitates our current focus on the border. But the threat posed is sometimes exaggerated for political gain, as are the size and scope of the current problem of illegal crossings. But in our most recent season of scapegoating, it is the dehumanization of vast groups of people based on nationality or ethnicity that is the worst of it. This dehumanization is the symptom of a bad impulse being surrendered to.

Growing up with migrant workers, I knew that they usually worked harder than we did. Sometimes my dad and my uncles would hire a few of my buddies from school to help with the harvest or the branding; they would last maybe a day or two and were often unreliable. But our Mexican migrant laborers worked hard, and we could count on them. Because of this experience, I have always said that I could never look at these migrants and consider them criminals. They were working to feed their families, and we simply could not have gotten along without them. So when during the 2016 campaign Jeb Bush committed a sin of candor by saying that people crossing the border did it as an act of love, well, that's exactly how I felt, too. And I said so at the time.

Having grown up with migrant labor and with the Hispanic community that was here long before we were, I knew that what Jeb Bush was saying was true. Among those who were raised in rural Arizona, it is much more difficult to summon the vitriol for immigrants that fuels so much of the politics in the age of Trump.

Of course, Jeb Bush was savaged for saying what he said, just mocked mercilessly. But then, unlike his critics, he knew what he was talking about and dared to speak truthfully, which is both a rarity and liability these days.

We have to return to the politics of comity and inclusion and reject the politics of xenophobia and demonization. But when there are so few contemporary examples of politics for the common good, where do we look for such a beacon?

I look to the people who raised me.

Cattle ranching is the hardest work I've ever known, and the best people I have ever known have been cattle ranchers. I was often asked as my father and his brothers aged if I had ever given any thought to taking over the operation. And by my answer I mean no false modesty: I am not smart enough to run a large cattle operation. There were many moving parts to the

F-Bar Ranch. You had to be an expert in biology, mathematics, accounting, animal husbandry, the commodities markets, marketing, meteorology, agriculture, business—probably psychology, too. My father did all of those things and still found the time to serve a term as mayor of Snowflake and work some twenty hours a week for free as the leader of our ward, or church congregation. It wasn't enough to work the land and build a business. You had to build community as well.

My great-grandfather, James Madison, was astute politically and followed the news well into his nineties. He'd press his one good ear to the radio and listen attentively. He had only one good ear due to having been shot by a desperado he and his brother were apprehending. Shot right through the ear. His brother, Charles Love Flake, was killed by the same bullet. This was the Snowflake of the 1880s, in the time of the Pleasant Valley Wars.

James Madison had to pitch in to help raise his brother's four children, and then within three years he lost his wife to illness and was left to raise nine kids of his own as well. At the time, he wrote in his journal: "Once again I must kiss the sod and face a cloudy future." That phrase sticks with me whenever I think I have it rough.

But life must be lived, and so James Madison married again; he would have a total of twenty-four children. In the early days of the twentieth century, he would take the time to honor his late wife, traveling around Arizona and as far away as Colorado to promote women's suffrage. On February 12, 1920, when Arizona ratified the Nineteenth Amendment, James Madison must have felt immensely gratified to have played his part.

Generally speaking, though, Mormons were cautious when it came to civic engagement, or with having much of anything to do with the state at all. There were the polygamy prosecutions of the late nineteenth century, for one thing, and indeed, my great-great-grandfather would endure six months of hard labor in a Yuma prison for having a second wife. But the primary reluctance was that we as a people had fled a government back east that wanted us dead, due to what it considered the "alienness" of our religion. Many Latter-Day Saints, taking this extermination order to heart, had soured on government altogether. Missouri Executive Order 44, which was signed by Governor Lilburn Boggs of Missouri in October 1838, read in part: "The Mormons must be treated as enemies, and must be exterminated or driven from the state if necessary for the public peace—their outrages are beyond all description. . . ."

One of those outrages, presumably, was Joseph Smith's vocal opposition to slavery, and the governor's executive order was the culmination of years of anti-Mormon sentiment, spurred by what were perceived as Joseph Smith's designs on taking over American civil society.

A manifesto written and signed by hundreds of Missourians, including elected officials, had preceded the extermination order, calling Mormons "a pretended religious sect," and "deluded fanatics."

Mormons, then, have had foundational and horrifying experience with some of these worst impulses of mankind and became both refugees and immigrants in our own land. And so when someone starts talking of religious tests and religious bans, we know better. Because we have seen this all before.

When we say "No Muslims" or "No Mexicans," we may as well say "No Mormons." Because it is no different.

That kind of talk is a dagger in the heart of Mormons. It is a dagger in my heart. Because we know firsthand that America was made great not by giving in to these impulses but by fighting them, and defeating them.

Governor Boggs's Mormon ban was officially on the books in Missouri for 138 years. Thankfully, cooler heads prevailed long before it was officially rescinded in 1976. But by that time, my family and most Latter-Day Saints had long since found refuge in a more welcoming location.

And that is how the Flakes came to Arizona.

But even as they established themselves in Snowflake and hundreds of places like it in the west, Mormons remained wary of the state, of the government, of the passions and prejudices of the day, and of politics. There was concern along the way that Mormons not let themselves become too concentrated on one side of the aisle or the other, and so church leaders in the late nineteenth century would go to wards—our word for congregations—and announce, "Those sitting on the left are Democrats and those sitting on the right are Republicans." This was to make sure that there was enough of a mix and that we engaged across the spectrum, that Mormons weren't put in a bad place should the prevailing political winds change.

In Snowflake, the instruction was that everybody who lived west of Main Street would be Republicans, and everybody east would be Democrats. The Flakes lived east of Main Street. (When my father met my mother, she gently informed him that his political inclinations were more aligned with the Republicans.) This political experiment struck me as bizarre when I was younger, but I have grown to appreciate the wisdom in it, too—the wisdom that says that before we are members of a party, we are people. Too often, labels prevent us from really *seeing* each other as such. Well, the Flakes listened in church, and we took this assignment to heart. There are to this day Flakes in town who have remained faithfully registered Democrats their whole lives and who are always up for a good argument at family gatherings.

This enforced ecumenical spirit didn't ever diminish my ardor for conservative policies or principles; if anything, it served to sharpen my arguments. But it did something else, too—it made me look for premises we could agree on. Out west, especially in rural areas, it has always been said that the citizen legislators know a lot more about working together than anybody in Washington ever did. Because you learn to count on your neighbors. The politics of consensus was the political culture I was weaned on, which is why this notion that you can simply choose not to work with the other side is foreign to me.

Politics is the art of persuasion. You've got to persuade people; you cannot compel them. Government is compulsion by definition, and it is the compulsion of free people that Goldwater stood against when he came along, turned Arizona Republican, and gave rise to the modern conservative movement. In this country, when we are at our best we argue vigorously, seek to persuade, have principles and defend them, but the things we do that have a chance of lasting—in law as in life—are the things in which every voice is heard. The toxicity of the moment we are in has been a long time coming, but it started when we decided that in order to succeed we had to silence and dehumanize each other.

By the time I ran for Congress in 2000, my Uncle Jake was in the state legislature. He ultimately served as Speaker of the House and then as a state senator, and he remains one of the most beloved figures in Arizona politics, regardless of party. He formed an alliance with Jack Brown, a Democrat from over in St. Johns, where the Udall family came from. Jack and Jake, two cowboy legislators, set aside party distinctions and let themselves be guided by common sense and common decency instead. They knew that there will always be issues that divide us. And some people, thriving on the division, work them like it's their job. But on the ranch, you have to get things done. Jake served in the state legislature until he died from injuries sustained from being thrown from his horse. A gentle cowboy to the end.

Prior to Jake, my second cousin Stan Turley served a turn as Speaker of the House, and he later became president of the state senate as well. He was cut from the same cloth, grew up in Snowflake, and lived under my grandfather's roof during his high school years because his folks lived too far out of town—too far for Stan to ride a horse to school every morning.

I attended Stan's funeral a couple of years ago, and found it remarkable. He was best known in politics for shepherding into law Arizona's groundwater code, which requires a hundred-year supply of water for any development to take place. That innovation is one of the reasons that, despite the severe drought we've been going through the past several years, Arizona remains well positioned, with an adequate water supply. We're in far better shape than California or other places in the west because Stan and a generation of rural lawmakers knew how to govern and get along. So at the funeral, here was this man who had spent years as Speaker of the House and as Senate president, but there was little mention of his time in politics. Rather, those eulogizing Stan remembered him, as they did my uncle Jake, for his character, his decency, his humor, and his sense of fair play.

The *New York Times* columnist David Brooks speaks of the desirability of "eulogy virtues" versus "résumé virtues." I've been given wonderful examples of the former all my life. I can only hope to be so remembered.

What is a conservative, exactly? And what is a conservative *not?*

Growing up, I didn't consider myself to be very political, nor did I expect that I would end up in politics. But my parents had eleven kids to feed—I don't remember ever going out to eat when I was young—so we spent a lot of time around the dinner table, and politics was often served. The importance of limited government, economic freedom, and individual responsibility were ingrained in our upbringing.

Peace, order, education, hard work, initiative, enterprise, cooperation, community spirit, patriotism, fair play, service to one's country, and honesty. These are all conservative values. Now, perhaps it is not allowed under the current rules of politics to say so, but I believe—and know from direct experience— that most liberals believe in these values, too. So what distinguishes a conservative? Well, that all comes down to the idea of government and its intersection with the lives of a free people. Conservatives recognize that there are limits to what government can and should do, that there are some problems that government cannot solve and shouldn't blunder into, and that human initiative is best when left unfettered.

Goldwater contemplated these philosophical propositions in ways both prophetic and timeless and applied them to the crisis of his day. His was a conservatism defined by freedom from government interference or coercion, and by the necessity for government to face hard truths and make hard choices, to be reliable and thrifty, and to not give in to the temptation to pander to populist sentiment while armed with a bag of money that doesn't belong to you:

> So it is that Conservatism, throughout history, has regarded man neither as a potential pawn of other men, nor as a part of a general collectivity in which the sacredness and the separate identity of individual human beings are ignored. Throughout history, true Conservatism has been at war equally with autocrats and with "democratic" Jacobins. The true Conservative was sympathetic with the plight of the hapless peasant under the tyranny of the French monarchy. And he was equally revolted at the attempt to solve that problem by a mob tyranny that paraded under the banner of egalitarianism. The conscience of the Conservative is pricked by *anyone* who would debase the dignity of the individual human being.

Goldwater continued, in a chapter entitled "The Perils of Power," to ask, "How did it happen? How did our national government grow from a servant with sharply limited powers into a master with virtually unlimited power?"

His answer:

> In part, we were swindled. There are occasions when we have elevated men and political parties to power that promised to restore limited government and then pro-

ceeded, after their election, to expand the activities of government. But let us be honest with ourselves. Broken
promises are not the major causes of our trouble. *Kept*
promises are. All too often we have put men in office who
have suggested spending a little more on this, a little more
on that, who have proposed a new welfare program, who
have thought of another variety of "security." We have
taken the bait, preferring to put off to another day the re-
capture of freedom and the restoration of our constitutional system. We have gone the way of many a democratic
society that has lost its freedom by persuading itself that if
"the people" rule, all is well.

This remains as true today as it was when published in 1960,
and even though the crisis as Goldwater saw it was different in
kind from the crisis we now face, what we have in common with
that senator from Arizona is the collapse of conservative principle, abetted primarily by people who describe themselves as
conservatives.

In his day, Goldwater saw the range of threats to liberty to
include autocrats at one end and those "democratic" Jacobins
on the other, with the true conservative equally at war with
each. But could Goldwater have contemplated the threat of au-
tocracy not from without but from within? Could he have foreseen a conservatism in America in the thrall of authoritarianism,
giving in to populism, throwing up barriers to free trade? And
how would he have responded?

As an Arizonan whose political philosophy was deeply informed by his, I have often thought, in answer to these and a
full range of pressing questions:

What Would Goldwater Do?

—Would he have thought that it is conservative to abruptly
    abandon the core conservative belief of free trade with

the world and break with multilateral trade agreements?
Or abandon established or pending trade deals, creating
a void in world markets that is currently being filled by
China, Russia, and even Mexico, just to name a few?

—Is it conservative to believe in the magical thinking that
suggests that we can ignore the growth in "entitlement"
spending simply by declaring that our growth rate will
reach at least 4 percent annually—growth that will make
the Social Security Trust Fund flush again?

—Is it conservative to play chicken with some of the most
productive and important international alliances we
have ever had?

—Is it conservative to heap praise on dictators and to
speak fondly of countries that crush dissent and murder
political opponents, and muse that the Chinese massacre
of students at Tiananmen Square "shows you the power
of strength"?

—Is it conservative to attack and undermine the intelligence agencies that are essential to our national security
and to attack their findings as "hoaxes"?

—Is it conservative to vilify religious and ethnic minorities?
To exaggerate threats and stoke security and economic
fears? To promise that another sovereign country will be
forced to pay for a border wall just because such a promise gets a good response at rallies?

—Is it conservative to embrace as fact things that are demonstrably untrue, to traffic in "alternative facts," and
to attack the constitutionally protected free press as the
"enemy of the people"?

—Is it conservative to propagate a conspiracy theory about
the birthplace of the president of the United States, long
after the facts have put the theory to rest? And is it conservative for members of Congress to remain silent as
such conspiracy theories are propagated?

—Is it conservative to undermine confidence in our democratic elections, to describe them as "rigged," and assert with no evidence that three to five million illegal aliens voted in the last general election?

Sadly, this list could be much longer. It is unpleasant to have to ask these questions. It is not easy to think about the current state of conservatism. But it is a conservative's responsibility to do so.

I certainly could never presume to answer those questions for Senator Goldwater, but for myself, I will resoundingly say *no* in answer to each. Emphatically: *No.*

It was to advance and defend conservative principles that I first decided to stand for election and get involved in public life. At that time, our national political duopoly was well established, and I had a pretty clear notion of who my political allies would be in this endeavor and, conversely, who my political opponents would be. And for the most part that dichotomy has held—until now. It is political unwindings such as we are now experiencing that scramble alliances and undo parties. But if I find myself here having to defend conservative principles against threats to those principles from people on my own side, well, it won't be the first time that that has happened.

Barry Goldwater was a famously crusty guy, albeit a good-humored kind of crusty. He was fearless, funny, and occasionally foul-mouthed. George Will once described him as a "cheerful malcontent," which is about right. In 1981, after President Reagan had nominated our fellow Arizonan Sandra Day O'Connor to be the first woman to serve as an associate justice on the United States Supreme Court, the evangelist Jerry Falwell had warned that "every good Christian should be concerned." Goldwater immediately responded that "every good Christian should line up and kick Jerry Falwell's #&*."

In 1992, after I became executive director of the Goldwater

Institute, I had the pleasure of receiving notes from Senator Goldwater. One congratulated me for a column I had written for the local paper, saying, "Ah, they're gonna come after you . . ." and for good measure he added a few four-letter words to describe whoever *they* were.

I had come to the Goldwater Institute after my church mission to southern Africa and after getting a bachelor's degree in international relations and a master's degree in political science from BYU. After school, I wanted to find work that would enable me to involve myself more deeply in the policy of developing nations, the kind of work that I had seen up close during my years in Africa. I searched for an internship on Capitol Hill, and it was one of my home-state senators, the Democrat Dennis DeConcini, who gave me a shot. Senator DeConcini had been active in Reagan-era policy in southern Africa, especially in arming Jonas Savimbi in Angola, who at the time was seen to be a freedom fighter, and as gratifying as my time in his office was, it almost cost me a job with the Goldwater Institute. I was by then an active Republican, but I was so naive that I had no idea that taking this internship with Senator DeConcini could henceforth brand me with a scarlet "D." When the Goldwater Institute board met to consider me for the job, it is my understanding that a few of the board members looked at my scant résumé and were heard to say, "He interned for a Democrat on Capitol Hill. What does he know about running a conservative, free-market think tank?"

By luck and grace and direct intervention by the Institute's chairman, Norman McClelland, I nonetheless got the job, and interestingly, not long into my tenure at the Institute, a press outlet in Arizona reported that "to critics, think tank leader Jeff Flake is considered a man of dark and dangerous ideas—a conservative 'extremist' on the way up." So, as I saw it—if I was making people on both sides uncomfortable, maybe I was where I needed to be.

I owe my chance to advance my "dangerous ideas" to an economist from the University of Arizona named Michael Block, who was president of the Goldwater Institute at the time. The staff back then basically consisted of me, so I started working immediately to try to build the Institute into a firmament of conservative ideas that would live up to the legacy of its namesake.

The Goldwater Institute had been founded in 1988 as one of many state-based free-market think tanks of the time, modeled after groups like the Cato Institute, the Heritage Foundation, and the American Enterprise Institute. Those national groups, especially Heritage, had had a profound impact on the Reagan administration, and it was from these groups that he had gathered his administration's intellectual firepower and much of his cabinet. These new institutes were meant to work similarly in the state capitols, too—laboratories in which to work on things like education reform, welfare reform, and tax policy at the state level.

I came on in 1992, when I was twenty-nine, and I would stay for seven years, until my first campaign for Congress. During that time, I learned about the intellectual underpinnings of conservatism—things that one does not typically pick up hog-tying calves in Snowflake, Arizona.

What came more naturally to me was building the organization, which would grow to be a formidable farm team for southwestern conservatives and political leaders. We initiated the Goldwater Award in my first year, meant to shine a light on one whose conservative example had changed the world, and invited Jack Kemp out to receive the inaugural prize. Senator Goldwater himself did the honors.

The next year we thought we'd go big and ask Margaret Thatcher if she'd come receive the Goldwater Award, and much to our surprise, she said yes. Again, Goldwater presented the award. To complete a conservative trifecta for the ages, William F. Buckley Jr. was on hand to emcee the evening.

Buckley was a conservative colossus, in whose debt every American who claims conservative pedigree remains to this day. He was every bit as courageous as Goldwater in advancing and defending conservative positions during a period when conservatism had been in retrenchment and decline. It is Buckley who taught us how a real conservative deals with extremism and paranoia and a burgeoning culture of disinformation in the ranks. The scale of what we are now experiencing is orders of magnitude different, because of the Internet, but it is not new.

In 1955, when Buckley founded *National Review,* there had never been anything like it in the country. Buckley's magazine became the vibrant intellectual center of American conservatism, and in the late 1950s it not only championed Goldwater's rise to lead the conservative movement (which would lead directly to Reagan's rise over the next two decades) but also counseled Goldwater on how to handle the extremists in his party at the time, particularly the members of the shadowy John Birch Society, ardent anticommunists who were probably best known for their elaborate conspiracy theories of communist infiltration.

As he would later recount in *Commentary* magazine, early in 1962, Buckley arranged a meeting at the Breakers Hotel in Palm Beach, where he and the conservative thinker Russell Kirk would attempt to persuade Goldwater to run against Lyndon Johnson in the coming presidential election. Seizing the party back from Nelson Rockefeller and the moderates was a top priority. Goldwater, made somewhat famous by the recent publication of *The Conscience of a Conservative*, was in town and had taken to disguising himself so as not to be recognized. He showed up at the meeting in "extravagantly informal garb," Buckley would write, seeming a bit shocked that a man would wear a cowboy hat and jeans to a business meeting.

Of course Goldwater would run in 1964, but that's not what he wanted to talk to Buckley and Kirk about. *Forget about Rockefeller for the moment, what is there to be done about those crazies in the John Birch Society?* he wanted to know. Goldwater said, "Every other person in Phoenix is a member of the John Birch Society. . . . I'm not talking about Commie-haunted apple pickers or cactus drunks, I'm talking about the highest caste of men of affairs."

A retired candy maker named Robert Welch had founded the group in 1958, and the society had really struck a chord among the far right. His anticommunism may have been a little *too* ardent, though, as he was quite certain that President Dwight D. Eisenhower was a "dedicated, conscious agent of the Communist conspiracy," and he believed that the United States government was "under operational control of the Communist party." As of the summer of 1961, Welch believed, the government was "50–70 percent Communist-controlled."

The Republicans had just shed themselves of the demagogue Joe McCarthy, which had been a painful episode for Goldwater, and all in attendance at the Breakers meeting immediately saw the problem with being associated with the Birchers, a group that was both growing in influence and attaching itself to Barry Goldwater as their presidential ideal more and more with each passing day. All were determined to make a statement of principle and "excommunicate" the Birchers. Kirk was of the opinion that Robert Welch was "a man disconnected from reality." As the Buckley biographer John Judis would write, "Buckley was beginning to worry that with the John Birch Society growing so rapidly, the right-wing upsurge in the country would take an ugly, even Fascist turn rather than leading toward the kind of conservatism *National Review* had promoted."

Buckley decided to launch a sustained attack in *National Review*, starting with a long article in the very next issue. In it, he wrote:

How can the John Birch Society be an effective political instrument while it is led by a man whose views on current affairs are, at so many critical points . . . so far removed from common sense? That dilemma weighs on conservatives across America. . . . The underlying problem is whether conservatives can continue to acquiesce quietly in a rendition of the causes of the decline of the Republic and the entire Western world which is false, and, besides that, crucially different in practical emphasis from their own.

In hindsight, Buckley's broadside was the beginning of the end for the Birchers. Goldwater seized the moment and readily associated himself with Buckley's position, writing a letter to the editor:

I think you have clearly stated the problem which Mr. Welch's continued leadership of the John Birch Society poses for sincere conservatives. . . . Mr. Welch is only one man, and I do not believe his views, far removed from reality and common sense as they are, represent the feelings of most members of the John Birch Society. . . . We cannot allow the emblem of irresponsibility to attach to the conservative banner.

The emblem of irresponsibility.

I cannot help but be struck by the echoes here, fifty-five years later. We can clearly see the parallels as well as the divergences. *National Review,* the premier conservative periodical of the day, did not embrace the paranoid and the conspiratorial in a paranoid and conspiratorial time. Rather, Buckley took the lead in tackling a terrible problem, a problem that, had it been allowed to fester and grow, could have been a threat not only to movement conservatism but also to civil society.

Look at how we are dealing with the same problem now. While William F. Buckley's magazine has continued to acquit itself well in describing the world as it is, in other precincts, rather than taking the principled and rather easy stand of endorsing reality—the bare minimum requirement for a conservative identity—we now have a far-right press that too often deals in unreality and a White House that has brought the values of Robert Welch into the West Wing.

The emblem of irresponsibility.

As a certain kind of extremism is again ascendant in our ranks, we could do well to take a lesson from that earlier time. We must not condone it. We must not use it to frighten and exploit the base. We must condemn it, in no uncertain terms.

As a conservative, I find it very useful to trace back to a time when we were simply better at this, a time before we so readily abandoned the principles that make us conservatives in the first place. Back to Jake's time and Stan's time, back to the time of my father. Back to Buckley's example, and Goldwater's, and Kirk's.

It will always be essential for conservatives to find energy and ideas by defining ourselves in opposition to the liberal impulse to find a government solution to every problem and the equally illiberal impulse to silence disagreeable speech.

But we must never shirk our obligation to examine ourselves, too. I include myself in this admonition. In that, I am reminded of the Book of Matthew: "And why beholdest thou the mote that is in thy brother's eye, but considerest not the beam that is in thine own eye?"

How did this conservative taste for extremism come about? How did we let it happen? I feel compelled to declare: *This is not who we are.*

Which begs the question: *Who are we, then?*

And what do we believe?

CHAPTER FIVE

ON FREE TRADE, NOT-SO-FREE TRADE, POPULISM, NATIONALISM, AND THE COLLAPSE OF WHAT WE BELIEVE IN

When a man unprincipled in private life, desperate in his fortune, bold in his temper, possessed of considerable talents, having the advantage of military habits—despotic in his ordinary demeanour—known to have scoffed in private at the principles of liberty—when such a man is seen to mount the hobby horse of popularity—to join in the cry of danger to liberty—to take every opportunity of embarrassing the General Government & bringing it under suspicion—to flatter and fall in with all the nonsense of the zealots of the day—It may justly be suspected that his object is to throw things into confusion that he may "ride the storm and direct the whirlwind."
—ALEXANDER HAMILTON, August 1792

I T WAS A TIME WHEN too many Americans were feeling tricked and abandoned and beaten down, despairing in the face of economic uncertainty and economic crisis and destabilizing economic change, when an impassioned disdain for the status quo across the political spectrum became a movement in search of a leader.

At such times, there is the temptation to look for a savior from the political class who might offer deliverance—or at least slogans of deliverance, which is the problem with looking for deliverance from politicians.

Never has a party so quickly or easily abandoned its core principles as my party did in the course of the 2016 campaign. And when you suddenly decide that you don't believe what had recently been your most deeply held beliefs, then you open yourself to believing anything—or maybe nothing at all. Following the lead of a candidate who had a special skill for identifying problems, if not for solving them, we lurched like a tranquilized elephant from a broad consensus on economic philosophy and free trade that had held for generations to an incoherent and often untrue mash of back-of-the-envelope populist slogans. Seemingly overnight.

Seemingly overnight, we became willing to roll back the ideas on the global economy that have given America the highest standard of living in history and lifted hundreds of millions of others from poverty all over the world.

Seemingly overnight, we became willing to jettison the strategic alliances that have spared us global conflict since World War II.

Seemingly overnight, we gave in to powerful nativist impulses that have arisen in the face of fear and insecurity over the swiftly evolving global economy.

Seemingly overnight, we stopped speaking the language of *freedom* and started speaking the language of *power*.

Seemingly overnight, reckless, outrageous, and undignified behavior became excused and countenanced as "telling it like it is," when it was actually just reckless, outrageous, and undignified.

Seemingly overnight, the word *globalist* became a grave insult among people in my party who also called themselves "conservative." I remember a right-wing blog post during my election to the Senate that said that I had "been seen in the company of globalists in Paris, France." *Quel scandale!* Globalist as opposed to what, exactly? A provincialist? A parochialist? A localist? In this country, we are less than 5 percent of the world's population. We are 20 percent of the world's economic output. And if we don't trade, we don't grow. Given the alternatives, I'll take the globalist moniker, thank you.

Seemingly overnight, we became defined not by the limitless aspirations of a free people but by our grievances and resentments and our lowest common denominators. Rather than leaning in to the economy of the future, this nativist vision would have us clambering to reclaim an economy of the past—an economy, by the way, that even if it were possible to somehow reconstitute would make no sense in the twenty-first century.

Why did we do that? And how did it happen? How did conservatives betray conservatism? Or worse: How did we embrace incoherence?

It will likely take historians decades to figure out why, exactly, but political expediency and self-justification are time-honored traditions in politics, and they offer a good place to start any serious historical analysis of this particular conservative crack-up. But in this chapter and the next, I will try my hand at writing a first draft of that history.

The quick answer: We did it because it was cheap and easy and the real world is hard and defending a principled position to voters is harder still.

In every political movement there is always evolution and drift. And there are also inflection points—the hinges of history, when big changes happen—political realignments, resource conflicts, civil rights struggles, industrial and technological revolutions, waves of global economic connectivity and upheaval.

All of these forces can set parties floating like continents away from or into each other—tearing them apart or forming new ones. Over the past century, we have even seen our two major parties reverse roles on some of the biggest issues America has ever faced.

But those transformations were gradual, organic to other tectonic social changes taking place at the time, and took decades, even generations, to play out.

During the campaign of 2016, on the other hand, committed lifelong free-market conservatives, with their fingers to the wind, took no time at all to dispense with principle and be reborn as "fair traders" or "populists." All in an effort to chase our own pied piper, who admittedly seemed expert at mapping the nation's anxieties. Adapting the happy talk of a charismatic outsider was a lot easier than explaining, defending, and persuading voters of the things we actually believed.

Conservatives love to mock liberals for offering "free stuff" from the government, but what was our 2016 campaign if not that?

In politics, it is difficult to win an argument with complexity and facts when the other side offers easy answers and free stuff without worrying about the details. This is largely how Donald Trump vanquished the Republican field in 2016. A tone that many of his supporters took for candor—*Our leaders are so stupid! I alone can fix it!*—combined with easy answers to hard questions, sweetened by free stuff. Candidate Trump was giving—and we, the Republican electorate, bought—the late-night infomercial: "Health Care for Everybody! Much Better, at a Fraction of the Cost! Free Border Wall! Super-Colossal Trade Deals! But Wait! There's More!!"

Free, yes. But also free of significant thought. The explanation for how the party of free trade went along with a candidate who came out against free trade—alternately describing himself as a free trader and a fair trader, eager for trade wars, threatening tariffs, calling for border taxes, and coming out against most multilateral trade agreements ever negotiated—is quite simple: We conservatives too often didn't have the courage of our convictions. Call us willing accomplices. The instant a flashy new novelty act came along, shredding conservative orthodoxy in the name of "telling it like it is," we bailed. The specter of winning arguments in the public sphere on the strength of our ideas proved too daunting.

I was heartsick when former free-market conservatives, in philosophical resignation, jumped aboard the populist bandwagon, turning the Republican Party into Trump's Party with reckless abandon. This transformation seems less a genuine instance of Saul on the road to Damascus than an example of *Oh, those core principles I've professed my entire career? Never mind!*

But as long as we are jettisoning the things we claim to believe most dearly, we may as well remind ourselves what those principles were—as a proper memorial, if nothing else. Or perhaps as a beacon for future generations who might be interested in what "American conservatives" once championed, and why.

I once had occasion to meet the eminent Chicago School economist Milton Friedman. A giant among conservatives, Friedman came to the Goldwater Institute one year in the 1990s to receive the Goldwater Award. We picked him up at the airport, and while were driving to a suburb of Phoenix called Ahwatukee, we went through what can only be described as suburban sprawl. Someone in the car with us, remarking on the landscape, said, "Man, it looks like there was no planning at all." Friedman just nodded his head and said, "Yes, isn't it beautiful?"

This was a classic Milton Friedman statement. Whatever the aesthetics of the suburban development, it wasn't government coercion that had brought it into being. It was the invisible hand of the free market that had sprawled such a community.

Planning requires control, control empowers government, and empowered government = disempowered individuals.

Friedman's musings out a car window are a pretty good distillation of what American conservatives used to believe. At least, it's what we professed to believe when we were safely among the herd.

Obviously, where private and public interests intersect, government has a role to play, and sometimes that role is robust. But free people, freely making decisions among themselves, with the government involved as little as possible—that is the essential conservative position, the fixed principle from which all negotiation starts, and against which all end results are measured.

As influential as Friedman remains, perhaps the more influential economic thinker for my generation of conservatives is the Nobel Prize–winning economist Friedrich Hayek, the only major recent member of the Austrian School actually born in Austria. Hayek's writings on government interference and government coercion—chiefly his epic *The Road To Serfdom*—became seminal texts for thinking conservatives from Margaret Thatcher to Paul Ryan (Speaker Ryan has said that he gives the book to new staff members to "bring them up to speed") and everybody in between. Such devotion has cemented Hayek's place in the conservative firmament. It was Hayek who went head to head with John Maynard Keynes, the collectivists, the socialists, and economic interventionists of all stripes during the seismic intellectual battles of the twentieth century. It was Hayek who wrote movingly of the "marvel" of free men and free markets and the prerogatives and industry of individual human beings and most persuasively against the dangers of the encroaching power of the state. It was Hayek who understood that liberty would be fleeting if the values of liberty were not continually reasserted.

For Hayek, the economy wasn't just another in a list of

issues that citizens considered and politicians exploited; *the economy* was all-encompassing, the whole shooting match. It was that to which all other "issues" are subsumed. It's not as if we depart the economy when we think about other issues, any more than a fish in the ocean thinks, "Okay, now I'm swimming. Maybe later, I'll do something else."

And so for Hayek, economics was the science of the elemental—as ubiquitous as air (or water) and as profound as Aristotle, involving itself in the mysteries of the human heart, the vicissitudes of human reasoning, and the majesty of free will. Hayek would live for almost the entire twentieth century, until 1992, just as the free market's triumph over the centrally planned economies was playing out so magnificently across the globe. As conservatives looking to buttress the moral and intellectual underpinnings of our beliefs, we can simply have no more formidable thinker in our corner than Hayek.

But we as conservatives would do well to read more deeply in Hayek, for it was also Hayek who, in an essay published in 1960 entitled "Why I Am Not a Conservative," wrote of two problems with conservatism in his day that could easily make him a prophet in ours: (1) conservatism's reluctance to accept evidence for "well-substantiated new knowledge" and (2) conservatism's tendency to give way to the corrupting influence of nationalism. Because nationalism, though understandable as a cultural and political phenomenon, is bad both for policy and for markets.

On the first point, Hayek was castigating the conservative mind's struggle with the theory of evolution, just as he might similarly castigate twenty-first-century conservatives over our reluctance to accept that the earth is warming. "By refusing to face the facts, the conservative only weakens his own position," he wrote. "Only by actively taking part in the elaboration of the consequences of new discoveries do we learn whether or not they fit into our world picture and, if so, how. Should our moral beliefs really prove to be dependent on factual assumptions shown to be incorrect, it would hardly be moral to defend them by refusing to acknowledge facts."

But it is on the second point that Hayek was most eerily prescient about the problems of conservatism in the twenty-first century: "Connected with the conservative distrust of the new and the strange is its hostility to internationalism and its proneness to a strident nationalism," he wrote.

> Here is another source of its weakness in the struggle of ideas. It cannot alter the fact that the ideas which are changing our civilization respect no boundaries. But refusal to acquaint one's self with new ideas merely deprives one of the power of effectively countering them when necessary. The growth of ideas is an international process, and only those who fully take part in the discussion will be able to exercise a significant influence. It is no real argument to say that an idea is un-American, un-British, or un-German, nor is a mistaken or vicious ideal better for having been conceived by one of our compatriots.
>
> . . . it is this nationalistic bias which frequently provides the bridge from conservatism to collectivism: to think in terms of "our" industry or resource is only a short step away from demanding that these national assets be directed in the national interest.

My Senate staff will attest that I routinely strike the word *our* when it appears in memos, letters, and speeches. "Our children" is the most offensive of these, as it so easily conjures up visions of a nanny state, and politicians take all manner of license to do just about anything in the name of "our children," and the same goes for "our seniors" and "our small businesses," which are almost as paternalistic.

Directing assets "in the national interest" is exactly the kind of misguided behavior that conservatives have always accused liberals of advocating. According to Hayek and central to conservative ideas of economic freedom for much of the past century, when free-market competition is corrupted with market controls and central planning, market outcomes are artificially impeded, competition is stifled, and the door is opened to all sorts of unintended downstream consequences. But in his essay eschewing conservatism, Hayek describes a *conservative* impulse so extreme that it poses the very same risk that conservatives have always warned against, and is but "a short step away" from that which conservatives most oppose.

It is obvious but worth repeating that patriotism and nationalism are distinct, if not opposing, ideas. While Hayek doesn't exactly concur with Orwell's notion that nationalism is "the great modern disease," he does see nationalism as a poisonous idea at its worst, leading to rash decisions in defense of national prerogatives or national identity that almost always make things worse—more akin to the collectivist/interventionist impulse than anything that coherent conservatives favor. The conservative philosophy—not just the conservative philosophy but the American philosophy—since World War II in particular is that America does well when everybody else does well. That has been the driving force behind our foreign policy as well as our trade policy for the past seventy-five years. The old adage holds true: When goods don't cross borders, guns do. Trade and the global expansion of capitalism have been central to conservative economic philosophy for as long as there has been a conservative movement.

But in 2016, nationalism merged with its cousin, populism, and suddenly there were winners and there were losers, trade was a zero-sum game, and enemies of the people were duly identified. The solution to our problems was to erect physical barriers between us and the world as well as metaphorical barriers between Americans, as populists will do. Our multilateral trade deals were suddenly the worst deals in the history of mankind, and other countries were benefiting and we had been left holding the bag—when in truth, all of the countries engaged in trade were doing better. Efficient and truly global supply chains mean that the component parts of an "American" car sometimes cross four or five borders—or our own borders four or five times—before that car rolls off the assembly line. Specialization, modernization, and mechanization mean a better standard of living for everyone and make for a more peaceful world as well. It wasn't clear if Donald Trump didn't believe any of this, or if he just hadn't thought very much about it.

By definition, conservatives don't blunder into complex and delicate systems that we don't understand and substitute our own judgment where the judgment of people who know what they're talking about is much more useful. More to the point, free-market conservatives don't presume to heedlessly interrupt the organic processes of the market, which Hayek likened to the natural processes found in biology or chemistry—sometimes hard to predict, sometimes brutal, but honest and beneficial in their outcomes when left to their own devices. For Hayek, the impulse to "order the unknown" and the view that "anything produced by evolution could have been done better by the use of human ingenuity" were completely untenable.

The same is true in an economy. I am sure that those who favor aggressive economic intervention mean well, but I believe, as Hayek did, that "deliberately trying to arrange elements in the order that we wish them to assume" is a fool's errand, and counterproductive. Meaning well and doing good are often opposites in outcome, and actually the most altruistic approach to take is not to try so hard to be altruistic but instead harness the natural forces of a free economy to far greater effect. "Good intentions will not suffice—we all know what road they pave," Hayek wrote in *The Fatal Conceit: The Errors of Socialism*, his last great work, in which he warned us about those who believe they can substitute their own judgment—politicians, bureaucrats, et al.—for the machinations of the free market. This impulse, he reasoned, is fatal to a market economy. Rather, to do good is to let the market do well: "The morals of the market do lead us to benefit others, not by our intending to do so, but by making us act in a manner which, nonetheless, will have just that effect."

This thinking has been central to the hard-headed, reality-based conservatism I have believed in my entire life. I would argue that it is the central idea of economic conservatism. I did not embrace free-market precepts because I value dogma for its own sake, or because I enjoy being doctrinaire, but rather because I believe that these ideas, tested by time, offer the most freedom and best outcomes in the lives of the most people. And as a constitutionalist, I believe that we have a clear guide of what government should and should not do.

Senator Goldwater's idea of government was similarly prescribed. I do not believe, for instance, that Goldwater was opposed to the Civil Rights Act of 1964 out of hostility toward civil rights. I believe he was opposed to the law because he thought that enacting such a policy wasn't a proper role of government and that economic and other social forces—the "society," independent of the government—would have eventually solved the manifold problems of racial discrimination. I have the benefit of historical hindsight, but this is an area of rare disagreement I have with Goldwater. I do so because in the case of civil rights for African Americans, the government itself was in fact an active agent of repression and was complicit in the denial of rights, as it had been for most of the century since emancipation. And so by the 1960s, it was a fit role of government to provide relief from an undeniably unjust situation, to neutralize the malignant influence of the whole of Jim Crow—which consisted of government policies—and rip it out, root and branch. When the institutions of government are a partner to injustice and are actually playing a malign role in making society unequal, then I am in agreement with the words of Chief Justice Earl Warren from his decision in *Brown v. Board of Education*: It must be stopped "with all deliberate speed."

Do we as a people and as a government sometimes need to ameliorate the most deleterious effects of capitalism? Should we extend a hand to the most vulnerable and to those most in need? Of course we should. We as a society have a compelling interest in doing that, both morally and in the exercise of what can be called enlightened self-interest. We must always be mindful of concentrated power, whether it be found in government or in business monopolies.

What makes the role of elected officials different from that of economists and academics is that academics are not responsible directly to the people—the real world is the real world and not merely an academic exercise. And when it comes to governance, the landscape shifts subtly over time, and sometimes the most unexpected outcomes come from the most unexpected places. President Kennedy, for instance, was inadvertently the original supply-sider, eighteen years before the Reagan tax cuts. Two years into his presidency, Kennedy observed that "it is a paradoxical truth that tax rates are too high today and tax revenues are too low." High taxes were depressing private investment in the economy, keeping the American standard of living lower than it should have been. And Kennedy's tax cuts—conceived and executed by New Frontier Keynesians—were as beneficial as Reagan's, resulting in an enormous increase in business investment and economic activity, which also financed a great many local and state government programs all over the country. It was Nixon who made the mistake of hiking the capital gains tax, which had a stultifying effect on the economy, only to be corrected, interestingly enough, when Jimmy Carter signed into law a massive capital gains tax cut, which resulted in an explosion of venture capital in the late 1970s.

Politics, then, is highly paradoxical. Any honest appraisal

of history shows us that it is not at all a zero-sum exercise and that the battle lines are seldom drawn straight. Some of the ideas in what became known as Obamacare were conceived by scholars at the Heritage Foundation as "conservative" ideas, and even Hayek was in favor of some form of what might be called universal health care. All of which is proof that conservatives can have honest differences of opinion on policy matters, among themselves and with others—or be open to entirely new ideas—without being thought heretical.

But there is a vast difference between policy and principle. One is infinitely negotiable, the other is not. Principles are not selective, preferential, temporary, or incoherent. Principles last, presidents do not.

There is no bigger bogeyman for conservatives than some liberal who wants to interfere in the market to "pick winners and losers." We have long been critical of the corruptions of the free market advocated by "progressives" and crony capitalists, and we've gotten a lot of mileage out of that "winners and losers" line.

Until 2016, that is.

As Emerson said, "An institution is the lengthened shadow of one man." I will add to that: Of no institution is this more true than the American presidency. Impulsive and lacking a coherent economic analysis, Trump moved beyond the election attempting to demonstrate his vaunted deal-making abilities. He promptly began to commit Hayek's fatal conceit, but with a twist that not even Hayek himself could have imagined: The new president would not merely demonstrate a preference for specific sectors of the economy, he would meddle in the economy by advocating for—or conversely, by intimidating—*specific companies.*

To conservatives, this is the essence of crony capitalism. For the conservative, the role of government is to create a conducive tax and regulatory environment and let the free market prosper. But if a president is incoherently intervening wherever he or she sees fit, it can only lead to bad things. President Trump would go on to propose the worst kind of uneconomic "deals" with the coal miners who so ardently supported him and believed his promises about the resurgence of an industry long in decline, but their old jobs really weren't coming back.

Virtually every public utility in the country had already made the market decision to move away from coal. Obama administration environmental regulations had certainly hastened these market changes, but abundant and cleaner natural gas was a larger culprit. One irony was that the most sustainable coal jobs involved coal for export—to trade with China.

But that didn't stop the president-elect from boasting of his deals and posing for his photo ops with Carrier air conditioner and Ford and other companies in efforts to thwart production facilities that those companies had planned to open in Mexico, and he would deride and threaten every multilateral trade deal either already struck or under negotiation.

It was a cruel fiction born of economic nationalism that ignored the complexity of the global economy and its increasingly interdependent supply chains and that seemed to miss how the American economy had evolved since the peak of manufacturing after World War II.

If America were to abandon multilateral trade agreements, either in fits of pique or in the vague hope of negotiating better bilateral deals, then China and other free-trading nations would rush in to fill the void, leaving America behind and doing lasting harm to our economic position and standing in the world. In an economy that moves at the speed of light, a trade policy made up primarily of nostalgia and tough talk would be devastating for the United States, doing irreparable damage to our wealth and standard of living.

But if this was a cruel fiction, all of us who called ourselves "conservative" were its co-authors. Rather than fighting the populist wave that threatened to engulf us, rather than defending the enduring principles that were consonant with everything that we knew and had believed in, we pretended that the emperor wasn't naked. Even worse: We checked our critical faculties at the door and pretended that the emperor was making sense.

The new president was playing on the understandable hopes and fears of people who were truly worried about their economic destinies and those of their children, and he was selling the impossible dream of reconstituting the American economy solely as an export economy, a sort of utopia where all trade agreements advantaged America first and America only. But instead of telling the truth and exhorting the American people toward the economies of the future rather than making them believe we could reclaim the economies of the past, we were party to a very big lie. Because, well, *look at his numbers!* He must be doing something right! In 2016, Donald Trump captured the imaginations of millions of Americans and laid waste to a crowded Republican field, dominating the American political scene like few figures in American history.

It is a testament to just how far we fell in 2016 that to resist the fever and stand up for conservatism seemed a radical act. It is a threshold requirement for a conservative to be able to both tell and expect the truth. We must demand and accept nothing less. Assuaging the public with happy talk quite obviously isn't a conservative thing to do. Viewing the government paternalistically isn't either.

Once a populist fever abates, truth must fill that void. But it is an ugly fact that the truth doesn't play well on the campaign trail. Free trade never fares well during campaigns. It's always easier for a politician to point at a shuttered factory and go looking for a scapegoat rather than tell the truth about modernization, mechanization, automation, and the more efficient allocation of capital—all things that have made our lives better. But those things are difficult to explain in a campaign.

But for those of us who have been elected, our job is to communicate, so we must communicate. We can't just pander and promise impossible things. Because the truth is that there is no easy solution to our changing economy. The truth is that we are producing about twice as much as we did in the 1980s with 30 percent fewer workers. The truth is that coal probably isn't coming back in our lifetimes, that auto plants that once employed hundreds will now only employ dozens, that automation has made our economy more productive than it has ever been. We will simply have to find a way to make sure that those who are just starting out are going into engineering instead of political science (my chosen major), and that if you're forty or fifty years old the future includes you, too, in a way that can provide a stable income and retirement. But it will be the future, not some rose-colored past. And it won't be easy. Anyone who tells you it's easy is not telling you the truth.

Granted, none of that is as catchy as "the American dream is dead and you're the victim of a rigged system." And none of that is as visceral as economic nationalism and fear—fear of the other, fear of national decline, fear of the future. In the 2016 election, a suffering American working class was ripe for Trump's message of fear, which was relieved to hear an easy solution that only he had thought of and only he could execute. Such a reductive populist message should make conservatives ill. But as this message advanced, we retreated, before capitulating altogether.

If brevity is the soul of wit, then former secretary of state George Shultz is a very witty man. In a brilliant, very brief piece published in *The Washington Post* in the spring of 2017, entitled "Everything You Need to Know About Trade Economics, in 70 Words," Shultz and Harvard economist Martin Feldstein tersely and elegantly described the real world and expressed the conservative position better than any of us had managed during the campaign the year before, when facts were hard to come by and ignorance was not a liability. The piece read:

> If a country consumes more than it produces, it must import more than it exports. That's not a rip-off; that's arithmetic.
>
> If we manage to negotiate a reduction in the Chinese trade surplus with the United States, we will have an increased trade deficit with some other country.
>
> Federal deficit spending, a massive and continuing act of dissaving, is the culprit. Control that spending and you will control trade deficits.

Globalization has occurred. That is reality. Free trade agreements didn't create globalization; they are a result of it. The question is, do we adapt to inexorable global trends and lead them as we have always done, maintaining our position as the largest and most innovative economy in the world? Or do we pretend that this hasn't happened, pretend that we can turn back the clock, pretend that we can reform the American economy as an export economy from the 1950s?

This was an open question in the immediate aftermath of the election of 2016, so powerful was the populist impulse that had taken hold in the country, so heated was the anti-trade rhetoric that seemed decisive in the pivotal states of the Upper Midwest.

Two weeks after the election of 2016, I visited Mexico City to meet with the foreign minister and several members of the Mexican legislature to discuss the relationship between our countries. Planned well before the election, the trip took on a new significance after it, as an uncertain new era was just beginning. Mexico is a vital trading partner to the United States, but it is particularly important to the economy of Arizona, and so I wanted to hear out the Mexican leaders and reassure them as much as I could.

During the campaign, candidate Trump had promised to "rip up" NAFTA, continually calling that trade agreement "the worst deal ever negotiated by the United States."

I would meet with several members of the Mexican Senate, the foreign minister, the minister of the interior, the secretary of the economy, and other trade and investment officials to discuss a full range of issues, including immigration and strategies for preserving free trade. I also met with the American ambassador to Mexico, Roberta Jacobson, whom I had helped to confirm over the objections of those who weren't happy that she had ably negotiated the agreement providing for a restoration of U.S.-Cuba diplomatic relations.

Since my election to Congress in 2000, I had been trying to end the travel ban to Cuba. Whatever utility the policy had once served, it had long since stopped making sense. But it still carried with it great emotional power, especially to the children and grandchildren of Cuban exiles, so I understood Senator Marco Rubio's reluctance to change the policy, even as I disagreed with him.

Opening Cuba, both to allow Americans to move freely and to influence the future of the island nation, seemed consistent with a freedom agenda. Either we mean it or we don't. Freedom is freedom, and that includes the most basic freedoms of personal agency: You get to choose where you can go, what you can do, and with whom you associate. And that means not hanging on to vestigial policies of the Cold War whose purpose was to punish despots in the distant past but that in fact punish no one more than the same people who were too long subjugated by the dictatorial regime. A double whammy. We meant well by it, and those who still support it mean well, but the Cuba embargo and especially the travel ban were ideas that had long since outlived their usefulness.

In 2005, I had the interesting experience of meeting former Polish president Lech Walesa, whose strike at the Gdansk shipyard starting in the early 1980s made him both a political prisoner and the David that slew the Goliath of the USSR's puppet regime in Warsaw. So Walesa's anticommunist credentials are impeccable. Near the end of our conversation, he told me that the Cuba policy of the United States made no sense to him. "You have a living museum of socialism in your backyard," he told me. "But why won't you let Americans visit the museum?"

There was no good answer to Walesa's question. Since I had backed efforts for nearly a decade to lift the Cuba travel ban, I decided to offer bipartisan support to President Obama's move to open Cuba again for Americans, in the stubborn belief that as a free American, if someone was going to tell me that I couldn't go to Cuba, it should be a communist Cuban dictator who is in the business of controlling peoples' lives and not an American president. Once President Obama initiated the new Cuba policy, American tourism and American dollars began to have a wonderfully corrosive effect on Cuban communism, and the effect of removing restrictions on remittances sent to relatives on the island from the United States would be even more profound, seeding the Cuban soil for private enterprise. Recently, the Trump administration announced that it will revive some of the old restrictions on the freedom of Americans to travel to Cuba. I can't help but think that Fidel Castro would be smiling. In life, he managed to restrict the freedom of Cubans. In death, he's somehow managed to restrict the freedom of Americans.

Ambassador Jacobson, who at that time was assistant secretary of state for the Western Hemisphere, had proven herself an impressive diplomat in that effort, and her mettle would certainly be tested in her role representing America in Mexico during what promised to be a fraught period.

There had been so much negative attention paid to the border during the campaign that I felt it important to make sure that the region remained a hub of commerce and not just a place with more Border Patrol agents. Over the past several years we had added infrastructure on our southern border, particularly the Mariposa Port of Entry at Nogales, and the Mexican government had made infrastructure commitments on its side as well. After years of harsh rhetoric and misguided legislation that resulted in boycotts of the state, Arizona's new governor, Doug Ducey, had established a trade office in Mexico City to better serve our state's interests, in recognition that Arizona conducts about $15 billion in trade with Mexico annually.

In Mexico City, much to my surprise, the officials I met with didn't take the much-discussed border wall very seriously. It was generally met with a chuckle. They seemed to appreciate the political theatricality of the "big, beautiful" centerpiece of the American presidential campaign. By then, in any case, more Mexican nationals crossing the border were heading south than were heading north. There was some concern about deportations—what constitutes a criminal alien, how they might be dealt with, and to where they might be repatriated. For example: Would America be repatriating only Mexicans to Mexico, or would we be trying to slip in other foreign nationals, too?

Preserving the trade relationship between our countries, however, was a matter of great concern to them, and as they considered the possibilities of what might happen, the one variable they could not predict was the new American president and what he might do. Their conclusion nonetheless was that our two countries were so inextricably intertwined economically that there was simply no way that NAFTA could be renegotiated expressly to "stick it" to the Mexicans without having it boomerang right back at the United States.

The integration of global markets has been a world-historic event, and along with extraordinary benefit it has admittedly brought some disruption as well—in industries, economies, and lives. Mexico has lost a lot of agriculture jobs, just as America has lost auto manufacturing jobs. It is vitally important that we acknowledge the pain that comes with change and answer it with practical solutions, such as vigorous training for the jobs of the future, particularly for those people and communities most directly affected. But those who seek to reclaim the past and see only the disruption and not the benefits of global economic connectivity are missing a larger truth of free trade.

And what is that truth? NAFTA created the largest free trade zone in the world, with an economic output of $20 trillion. It quadrupled trade between the three countries, quadrupled American exports to Canada and Mexico, eliminated tariffs that had increased the cost of doing business, and reduced prices for consumers. NAFTA also reduced American dependence on Middle Eastern oil, created many more jobs than it eliminated, and fostered new markets for investment by American companies. Yes, some American manufacturing jobs have been lost since 1994, the year that NAFTA was adopted, many of them to Mexico. But it is important to realize that most of those jobs would otherwise have gone to China, and in fact NAFTA may well have stanched some of the bleeding that we have experienced in the manufacturing sector of our economy. By integrating supply chains across North America, preserving a significant share of production in the United States became an option for manufacturers, especially manufacturers of complex consumer goods like cars. Before NAFTA, the United States was facing the wholesale decline of automobile manufacturing jobs.

A president who had campaigned against NAFTA as "the worst agreement ever" but spared the public the precise details of his thinking—well, he might do just about anything once elected.

With proper notice, he could simply withdraw from it. The effects of a move like that would be seismic. The United States would be seen as an unreliable trading partner and other countries would increasingly hesitate before entering into free trade agreements with us. If they believe that American leadership is mercurial and the agreements aren't going to endure, they'll understandably go looking for a more reliable trading partner. Further, if American companies believe that we've grown hostile to free trade agreements, they may well be inclined to move to countries that have more robust trade relationships. A president can talk all he wants about tearing up trade agreements and forging bilateral trade agreements, but given the nature of supply chains and value chains worldwide today, those are increasingly difficult to negotiate. Multilateral trade agreements simply reflect the world as it is now, and it is outdated thinking to pretend otherwise.

The rest of the world isn't waiting for us anymore; they're moving ahead. While I was in Mexico City, the Mexican secretary of the economy, Ildefonso Guajardo Villarreal, informed me that he had just been in Chile and Peru for trade meetings, and that the president of the People's Republic of China, Xi Jinping, and Russian president Vladimir Putin had been there at the same time, with the Chinese delegation boasting that they were "open for business." Xi also visited Ecuador during the same trip, spreading the word that "if the U.S. isn't moving in, then we are." We stand to be left further and further behind. We simply cannot afford four years of watching China move ahead.

And if President Trump didn't want companies to move to Mexico, he was saying precisely the wrong things. As it began to prepare for all contingencies for dealing with Washington in the Trump era, the Mexican government would whisper that if Trump were to succeed in pulling out of trade agreements without negotiating new ones, either multilateral or bilateral, it would undoubtedly result in *more* American companies relocating to Mexico in order to use Mexico as a trade platform to reach other markets, as Mexico has free trade agreements with more than twice the number of countries the United States does. As most things are, this issue is considerably more complicated and requires deeper thought than an early-morning tweet about a border tax might allow.

During my entire time in Mexico City after our election, the Mexican Senate was debating another much-maligned multilateral trade agreement that would have involved eleven countries—the Trans-Pacific Partnership—just as our president-elect announced that the United States would be exiting the agreement. That action rendered the Mexican Senate debate moot, which was deeply unfortunate. In the complex supply chain between the United States and Mexico, some of the auto parts that we manufacture jointly with Mexico cross the U.S.-Mexico border eight times during the manufacturing process. Eight times. And 40 percent of all Mexican "exports" are made up of American content. *40 percent.* So the notion that you can knock globalization and reduce these complex transactions to just "exports" or "imports" on some kind of economic nationalist scorecard is naive at best.

Free trade is a lift-all-boats phenomenon, and that is precisely what free-market economics is all about. It provides for the most efficient use of capital, because it doesn't make sense for us to manufacture certain widgets when other countries can make them faster and cheaper. It is precisely because we have taken advantage of globalization that we have the standard of living that we have. The TPP would have opened this supply chain to markets in Australia, New Zealand, and Vietnam, but that effort at advancing the good that capitalism can do was swamped in the populist bilge that flooded in from both the right and the left in the misbegotten election year of 2016.

If one were to actually talk to the Mexican government, as I did, and ask its representatives whether it might be possible to modernize NAFTA, they would respond eagerly. (You bet it is, is what they said.) It was an agreement that was negotiated more than twenty years ago. Intellectual property was not properly addressed. The energy sector was largely left out. There are many improvements that can be made to NAFTA, and the irony is: The Trans-Pacific Partnership actually made some of the precise modifications to NAFTA that we most needed. This was not something that was considered or discussed by the "rip it up" crowd.

Forty-eight hours before Donald Trump was inaugurated as the forty-fifth president of the United States, I met with Michael Froman, who was in his last forty-eight hours as the United States Trade Representative. Our meeting would be, he told me, his last visit to Capitol Hill as USTR. When I heard that that would be the case, I told Froman, "Great, then this is the meeting that'll put TPP over the top." Of course it wouldn't be, but a free-trader can dream, can't he?

The purpose of my meeting with our trade representative was to get his perspective on what the incoming administration could and could not do to existing American trade agreements without violating them or running afoul of the World Trade Organization.

That, of course, was before the new president began, in the spring of 2017, to threaten to withdraw the United States from the World Trade Organization, too. As John Brinkley in *Forbes* wrote at that time, "It's astonishing that our president and his commerce secretary, Wilbur Ross, believe that protectionism and economic isolationism are the yellow brick road to a renaissance of American manufacturing. It's amazing that they don't know that every administration that has walked that road has found that it leads to higher unemployment and lower economic growth."

What seemed to set President Trump off most was the trade

deficits that the United States carried with many countries, and in that he seemed to misinterpret what a trade deficit even is—assuming that if a country carries a trade deficit that it is somehow "losing" to the country with the trade surplus. And that this "losing" is always the result of bad trade deals struck by bad, "stupid" leaders.

But trade deficits are not always bad. For instance, the United States imports a lot more oil from Saudi Arabia than we make up for in the value of the goods we export to them. But it's still an exceedingly good deal for us, even though we run a perpetual trade deficit with the Saudis. And in terms of our relationship with Mexico, if one listened to the president's public scolding of American businesses, it would be easy to think that the only reason companies would relocate to Mexico would be to take advantage of cheaper labor. But sitting in my office on Capitol Hill on the cusp of a new administration, Mr. Froman told me that this was a fallacy, that labor was only a small part of the equation, and that free trade and freer access to world markets was a much bigger consideration for companies.

More and more auto manufacturing was leaving for Mexico—Audi had just gone there, rather than locating in the United States—and when the manufacturers are asked why, the answer is not cheaper labor—for the labor differential only accounts for about $600 per car between the United States and Mexico. So labor costs weren't driving the trend. The true answer was that Mexico was more of a platform for market access because of its greater number of free trade agreements—*that* advantage amounted to as much as a $2,400 difference per car. The reflex to slap tariffs on auto parts that are manufactured in Mexico and assembled here missed the point of what was driving companies out of the United States and misunderstood the complexity of capitalism and trade in the twenty-first century. By 2017, the United States was the second-biggest exporter in the world, but exports accounted for only 12 percent of our economy, which is still the biggest economy on earth. So market access to the rest of the world is vital.

That's the real tragedy of TPP's collapse. There will not only be economic consequences; there will be geopolitical and strategic consequences as well. In order to grow, we must be aggressive and progressive in terms of trade, and we must keep the countries included in the TPP in our trade orbit and not lose them irretrievably into China's trade orbit. Were that to happen, it would be to the detriment of the American worker for a very long time to come.

If there is a vacuum, the Chinese will fill it. Particularly with Southeast Asian countries that are growing and very much want to strike trade deals with us. If the United States draws the shades and nails up a sign that says CLOSED UNTIL FURTHER NOTICE, these countries will simply go elsewhere. By the spring of 2017, they already were doing so. This part of trade economics is not at all complicated. That may well be the greatest danger of viewing trade as a zero-sum game and every relationship as adversarial—the punch you throw will more than likely strike your own face.

Would the United States continue to champion free trade? In an extraordinary move, in Mr. Trump's first spring in the White House, it was reported that the president's own advisors would prevail upon the Canadian prime minister Justin Trudeau—a foreign head of state—to ask the president of the United States not to abandon NAFTA and instead take the more measured approach of renegotiating the agreement. Around the same time, as if to signal the embrace of incoherence at the highest levels of American leadership, the president referred to himself at one point as "both a nationalist *and* a globalist," a statement that certainly challenges most of our ideas of logic. So was America at the dawn of the Trump era a hospitable place for conservative notions of free-market capitalism? Were we for NAFTA or against NAFTA? The answer to those questions depended on the day, sometimes the hour.

Meanwhile, the world turned. Capitalism waits for no man.

It is perhaps the greatest vexation of our times that these pots were all being stirred by a person who described himself as a "conservative" and was embraced, or at least tolerated, by conservatives. Far from conservative, the president's comportment was rather a study in the importance of conflict in reality television—that once you introduce conflict, you cannot de-escalate conflict. You must continually escalate. That was an important principle of his campaign, and it defined at least his early approach to governing, too.

The easy abandonments of principle, to which all conservatives were party, had set conservatism adrift. The question is: Will enough of us stand up and wrest it back before it is too late? Or will we just go along with it, for our many and varied reasons? Those are open and unresolved questions.

What wasn't open and unresolved is what a conservative is and what a conservative isn't. A conservative isn't inconstant, mercurial, and shallow. Conservatives have a deep and abiding respect for order, but conservatives do not genuflect to power. Conservatives do not change their governing philosophy depending on fashion or the passions of the day or based on how much applause a line in a speech received at a rally.

CHAPTER SIX

HOW DID THIS HAPPEN? (OUR FAUSTIAN BARGAIN)

I N THE SPRING OF 2017, during the apex of our greatest political dysfunction, the secretary of defense, former marine general James Mattis, was asked by Dexter Filkins, a writer for *The New Yorker,* what worried him most. Unexpectedly for a man in his position, he said this: "The lack of political unity in America. The lack of a fundamental friendliness. It seems like an awful lot of people in America and around the world feel spiritually and personally alienated, whether it be from organized religion or from local community school districts or from their governments."

A few years before, one of Secretary Mattis's predecessors at the Pentagon, Secretary Bob Gates, had also been asked to identify the greatest threat to American national security. Like Mattis, Gates answered not by discussing Islamic jihad or a rising China or any number of other areas of geopolitical concern and instead said this:

> I think the biggest threat to our future sits in Washington, D.C., and not someplace else. The rest of the problems of

the world wouldn't worry me if we had a functional government. And if we had a Congress that could begin to address some of the long-term problems that the country has. I mean, the reality is our problems are deep enough in every category that none of them can be resolved during the course of one presidency or one Congress. So you need bipartisan solutions that can be sustained through more than one presidency and more than one Congress. And we don't see any evidence of that in Washington.

There you have it. Politicians who don't do their jobs are an actual threat to national security. These two wise men—who were as well versed via daily classified briefings into the inventory of actual enemies of liberty as any Americans—each independently identified his greatest worry and our gravest threat to be, essentially, ourselves. That should have been enough to make us all vow to cease this nonsense. But that would require both wisdom and courage, and these days, the political class in Washington seemed to possess neither.

It is one of the great paradoxes of our time that the nastiness and dysfunction that weakened the American will and softened the ground for the extraordinary election of 2016, rather than being remedied by the election, only begat more nastiness and dysfunction in the election's wake. It's as if we as a political culture had an irresistible morbid curiosity to see for ourselves just how bad we could be. An urge to the extreme, just to see what it's like. But the truth is, this slide into political entropy was a long time coming.

Before the collapse of conservative principle came the collapse of any semblance of a functional national politics. And if our failures of principle were manifest, our political failures, too, ranged from the prosaic to the extraordinary and everything in between. Seeking advantage over our opponents, we poisoned

the civic fountain from which we all drink, with predictable results.

In that, I am not blameless.

Any honest accounting of how this happened—of how we
made ourselves so susceptible to rank demagoguery and of how
we were accessories before, during, and after the fact to the collapse of conservative principles—must begin with me. To re-
trace the footsteps along the long path that led us here, we have
to be strong enough to be self-critical.

So let that begin with me.

Allow me to set the scene. (I even have a contemporaneous
written record of at least one of my offenses—call it an exhibit
in the case against me.) It was October 2008, a month before
the election, and at issue was the impending collapse of the
global economy. I was in my fourth term in the House, and at
the time I made it my business to be about as ideological as I
could possibly be. In fact, I relished doing so. Let other people
take the hard votes, I thought. Let somebody else carry my
water. I would choose to protect my sterling voting record
against egregious spending rather than do what I knew the
country needed in a time of unparalleled crisis. The first vote
on a $700 billion emergency bailout package had failed in the
House of Representatives, instantly causing the stock market to
drop 7 percent. This was a crisis that our parents who lived
through the Great Depression may have recognized but was entirely unfamiliar to people of my generation.

If there was ever a time for a pragmatic response, this was
it. With the Congress having no choice but to act, the bill
was scheduled for a second vote. Both of the presidential
candidates—Senators McCain and Obama—had agreed to put
politics aside and were supporting the emergency action very
publicly. Senator McCain was privately lobbying Republicans
to join him. He was especially leaning on the rebellious sorts in
the House like me, who had voted no the first time and were

planning to do the same thing again. One of my diary entries from the time:

Washington Update—October 3, 2008

"Jeff, John McCain here," said the voice on the other end of the line. "Hello, Senator," I said as I exited the cloakroom with the cell phone on my ear. It was Friday afternoon, and the second House vote on the bailout package was to occur within an hour or so. It was my fourth call in almost as many days from the would-be President. "Fancy hearing from you again."

"Well, have you changed your mind on the bill?" he said, getting down to business.

"I'm afraid not, John. I'm still voting no."

"Why you little jerk!" he said, not too convincingly. "Ah, ya know I love ya, Jeff."

"If it makes you feel any better, they've got the votes without me," I offered. I think he knew it by then. He was just trying to improve his batting average. I'd like to think he respected my position. In fact, I'm quite sure he'd be with me if he weren't running for President. It made me feel better to think so, anyway.

So, was this an easy vote? Being asked to spend $700 billion in taxpayer money to bail out banks and businesses whose poor business practices put them in the predicament they're in? It should have been easy, but, to tell you the truth, it wasn't.

That diary entry from that fateful week significantly underreports the trouble we were in as a country and the spillover effects into the global economy. Not only that, my critique focused only on the Wall Street scoundrels and not their Main Street victims should the federal government do nothing in the face of global calamity. Two weeks earlier, on September 18,

Treasury Secretary Hank Paulson and the chairman of the Federal Reserve, Ben Bernanke, had raced to the Capitol Building for an emergency meeting with the congressional leadership. The economy was in free fall, they said. Capital was seizing up all over the world. Without emergency liquidity, banks would fall like dominoes, savings would be wiped out, the global economy would be plunged into depression. Panic would ensue.

"Unless you act," Secretary Paulson told the assembled members of the House and Senate, "the financial system of this country and the world will melt down in a matter of days."

"If we don't do this tomorrow," Chairman Bernanke added, "we won't have an economy on Monday."

That was on a Thursday.

In that heady moment, a $700 billion behemoth called the Troubled Asset Relief Program was born. Better known as TARP, no bigger waste of taxpayer money had ever been conceived in the history of the republic—unless you counted the many multiples of that sum that Washington might end up shelling out if the bailout bill failed.

TARP was actually a modest price to pay to forestall a global depression. My vote against the bill is a vote that I still regret. That the vote did not hurt me politically is immaterial. That the bill was attacked from both right and left, and as a matter of policy was deeply flawed, is beside the point. Here's what mattered: At a moment of national and global crisis, that vote was an abdication of my responsibility as a member of Congress.

Yes, my vote was defensible as a critique of both the gross irresponsibility of the industries involved and the proper limits on government market interventions. Yes, it was consistent with my voting record, because I never voted for that kind of extraordinary spending. For example: In 2003, when I was a member of the House, the White House and the congressional leadership pressed Republican members to vote for the Medicare Part D prescription drug benefit bill. In my view, that bill was a cynical vote-buying exercise by Republicans—a benefit we could tout to seniors, who vote, while sending the invoice to their grandkids, who don't—the kind of generational theft all too often practiced on Capitol Hill. When Tom DeLay was whipping the votes for the bill, he came to me and asked, "I understand that you want to vote against this, but if it comes down to your vote being the deciding vote, certainly you won't be the one who sinks it, right?"

"Please put me in that position," I answered. "I would love to be known as the one who sank this boondoggle."

But Senator McCain's entreaty during those tense days in early October 2008 was very different from DeLay's proposition five years earlier. My TARP vote was more an act of cowardice than conscience. I knew what needed to be done. I just left it up to my colleagues to do it.

Long before the politics in Congress had reached its present level of toxic dysfunction, there had been a practice among members known as "vote no, hope yes," which is just like it sounds—vote one way, and hope the outcome, and the resulting policy, goes against you. The goals of this practice could be many—to stay at the top of various ideological scorecards, to make a show of party loyalty, to avoid a hard vote, to use your opponent's hard vote against him. None of the reasons was worth the dignity that was sacrificed in the bargain. Voting no but hoping yes is not governing in good faith; it is the antithesis of accountability. I was an occasional practitioner of voting no and hoping yes. That's what my TARP vote was.

When the bill came back for a second vote, several fellow Republicans—including my very conservative colleague from Arizona, John Shadegg, whose father had been Senator Goldwater's campaign manager—changed their votes to yes. Just as I should have done. Instead, I relied on Congressman Shadegg and others to do the dirty work for me.

Since my first election to Congress, it had always been a great source of pride and strength for me to try to put the interests of taxpayers first. Responsibility for the nation's purse had been and remains my north star. It is why I led in the effort to eliminate earmarks from our spending bills (much to the consternation of many of my colleagues from both parties), and it is why I believe that holding a conservative line on the growth of federal agencies, the federal budget, and the national debt is the most important part of my job. I take a back seat to no one when it comes to fiscal conservatism.

But maintaining one's ideological purity for political reasons, as I did that October day in 2008, is neither principled nor conservative.

If it is in your capacity to prevent great harm and ameliorate great suffering, what do you do? Do you spend the time, as the precious seconds tick away and the shadow of the tsunami darkens the land, blithely observing, "I told you not to build there," or do you rush to mitigate the disaster and save as many innocents as possible? The answer to that question depends on whether the requirements of politics have blinded you to the practical costs of inaction or not. The answer to that question depends on whether you're a leader or not.

The better path, always, is to break out of rigid ideological thinking, to listen to reasoned arguments on both sides, and to use your best judgment. (Observers of the political and civic situation in America today might think that the previous sentence was an attempt at humor. It was not.) It is important to know enough to be able to discern the difference between a standard political fight and a dire emergency. Thankfully, in 2008, a sufficient number of politicians on both sides of the aisle did the right thing. (A few years ago, when I first decided to run for the United States Senate seat being vacated by Jon Kyl, I vowed that never again would I vote no and hope yes.)

But our destructive politics would continue. And out political culture would grow even more coarse, and even less human.

In January 2011, a few days after Democratic Congresswoman Gabby Giffords was shot and gravely wounded while greeting constituents at a Tucson supermarket, we in the Arizona congressional delegation left an empty seat for her at that year's State of the Union address. That year, the delegation made it a point to sit together in solidarity rather than divide along party lines as the rest of the chamber typically does during the speech.

One year later, when Gabby—who was working very hard on rehabilitating from her grievous injury—returned to Congress, I sat next to her during the State of the Union. During President Obama's applause lines, Gabby wanted to stand up but was unable to do so on her own, so I helped her. That often left me standing, a lone Republican among cheering Democrats.

During and after the president's address, I received furious text messages and emails from partisans who wanted to know why I "agreed with President Obama."

I did not agree with President Obama on much during that speech, but Gabby Giffords was my friend, and it was my honor to help her stand that evening. It was a gesture of affection and decency for a cherished and brave colleague. I hadn't given it any more thought. It certainly didn't occur to me that I should worry what Republicans might think, because life is too short to worry about such things. In that moment, Congresswoman Giffords and I were not members of different political parties—we were friends, fellow Arizonans, fellow Americans, fellow human beings. And yet, all some people could see was that I was somehow consorting with the enemy.

Much the same thing happened in the late summer of 2016, on the day that my Democratic colleague from Virginia, Senator Tim Kaine, was added to the Democratic ticket as the vice-presidential nominee. Tim and I had entered the Senate together, and we obviously disagreed on many things, but I knew him to be exceptionally smart, hardworking, and patriotic. His son Nat was a Marine, on active duty. By way of congratulating Tim on being named to the Democratic ticket, I tweeted a playful jab: "Trying to count the ways I hate Tim Kaine. Drawing a blank. Congrats to a good man and a good friend."

Once again: remarkable, unhinged fury from the ideologues. At a political gathering not long afterward, I received a scolding from a die-hard Republican who felt that I was aiding and abetting the enemy: "If you can't say anything bad, don't say anything at. . . ." He caught himself before fully reversing the advice I'm sure his mother once gave him. Such is the conditioned response of a shattered politics.

Six years after Congresswoman Giffords was shot, I found myself in an eerily familiar setting—a hospital waiting room, listening as doctors described the critical condition of another colleague, Congressman Steve Scalise, who was fighting for his life after receiving a large-caliber gunshot wound to the hip. Four other victims were being treated for gunshot wounds on different floors and at different hospitals.

It was an early morning in June 2017, and this one hit even closer to home. We had all been practicing for one of the rare moments of comity in Washington—the congressional baseball game—when a crazed gunman opened fire. Arriving back at the Capitol later that morning in a daze, I carefully navigated my way across marble floors to the Senate gym in steel baseball cleats, because my gear was still in the dugout, which was by then a crime scene. As I changed out of my uniform, the red stains on my pant leg and a blood-soaked batting glove, used to apply pressure to Scalise's wounds, reminded me how fortunate I had been.

To discover later that the motive had been political was shocking. The gunman looked out on a ballfield and saw not a couple dozen middle-aged members of Congress taking batting practice. He saw the enemy.

It seems elementary to have to form this thought, much less write these sentences, but here we are: I am a proud conservative and a lifelong Republican. That does not make the Democrats my enemies. America has too many real enemies to indulge such nonsense. We ill serve the American people when our tribal impulses take over and we cease to have human responses to each other. When we have governed best, we have sought comity and consensus. We fight and argue vehemently for our positions and our principles, understanding that policies that last always bear the imprint of both sides. That is when America is at her best. And when we are at our worst, well, we reach the point where we are today.

The politics that would culminate in the election of 2016 was a politics of our own creation. This politics was a generation in the making and would force us to our corners, from which we would regard those who believe differently from us not merely as our political opponents but as our sworn enemy. Other *Americans*—the enemy. How does one accede to governing with the enemy? And will one's base stand for it?

Each side points its finger at the other for this pathetic situation, and each can cite evidence to support the claim. It was the Democrats who destroyed regular order in the Senate and debilitated the committee process, but it was Republicans who regularly played chicken with the full faith and credit of the United States.

When Democrats had a lock on Congress for generations, they wielded the redistricting map like a weapon, ensuring that they would always own Congress. Then the Republicans did the very same thing, so egregiously that the courts had to step in. When a state such as Pennsylvania has a little more than half of its voters voting for Democrats in the 2012 House races, yet has thirteen Republicans in its House delegation to only five Democrats, it seems certain that something is amiss. Similarly, in Maryland, where Democrats control redistricting, there are seven Democrats and only one Republican. Take a look at Maryland's Third District, said to be America's most gerrymandered. That tortured, twisted shape is what democracy looks like when it's being strangled.

Innovations in the collapse of governance have certainly been a bipartisan affair. The Democrats were the first to block a president's executive calendar for no reason other than to obstruct a president they didn't like—in that case, George W. Bush. Republicans returned the favor with Barack Obama, for similarly compelling reasons. This trend culminated most famously with the death of Supreme Court Associate Justice Antonin Scalia. Before sunset on the day of Scalia's death—February 13, 2016—it was announced that there would be no hearings on a Supreme Court nominee for the remainder of the Obama presidency, almost a full year. Even though the Republicans felt entirely justified in doing this, and even though the move was not entirely without precedent, we will almost certainly see a day when the Democrats do the very same thing. And so it goes.

Republicans can claim impressive contributions to the modern phenomenon known as the "politics of personal destruction," particularly with the rise of Newt Gingrich and his heirs—subordinating the concept of governing to the necessity of winning and wielding power. What all this winning and power were in the service of was sometimes hard to discern. Democrats proved to be very capable at this game as well, even to their own side when the target is thought insufficiently doctrinaire.

And the dehumanization of our politics continued, with democracy devolving downward all the while.

Gamesmanship replaced statesmanship. It has become a

cynical cliché that once in America voters chose their leaders, but now leaders choose their voters. Special census tract software called Maptitude enables partisan warriors to hijack the redistricting process to carve the country up into 435 of the most ideologically extreme expressions of the American polity, then "playing to the base" becomes the primary imperative, and compromise becomes disincentivized and thus nearly impossible. Somewhere along the way, the two parties lost the skills or the interest to talk to each other, gridlock seized the gears of government, despair was followed by rage at our collapse into chaos. We had reduced the majesty of these noble institutions to a tawdry numbers game, a game where the citizens lose every time. Obscured in the process was the notion of the common good as well as the concept of the "loyal opposition," that mainstay of American discourse and self-governance since the beginning.

Who could blame the people who felt abandoned and ignored by the major parties for reaching in despair for a candidate who offered oversimplified answers to infinitely complex questions and managed to entertain them in the process. With hindsight, it is clear that we all but ensured the rise of Donald Trump.

I will let the liberals answer for their own sins in this regard. (There are many.) But we conservatives mocked Barack Obama's failure to deliver on his pledge to change the tone in Washington even as we worked to assist with that failure. It was we conservatives who, upon Obama's election, stated that our number-one priority was not advancing a conservative policy agenda but making Barack Obama a one-term president—the corollary to this binary thinking being that his failure would be our success and the fortunes of the citizenry would presumably be sorted out in the meantime. It was we conservatives who were largely silent when the most egregious and sustained attacks on Obama's legitimacy were leveled by marginal figures who would later be embraced and legitimized by far too many of us. It was we conservatives who rightly and robustly asserted our constitutional prerogatives as a coequal branch of government when a Democrat was in the White House but who, despite solemn vows to do the same in the event of a Trump presidency, have maintained an unnerving silence as instability has ensued. To carry on in the spring of 2017 as if what was happening was anything approaching normalcy required a determined suspension of critical faculties. And tremendous powers of denial.

I've been sympathetic to this impulse to denial, as one doesn't ever want to believe that the government of the United States has been made dysfunctional at the highest levels, especially by the actions of one's own party. Michael Gerson, a conservative columnist and former senior advisor to President George W. Bush, wrote, four months into the new presidency, "The conservative mind, in some very visible cases, has become diseased," and conservative institutions "with the blessings of a president . . . have abandoned the normal constraints of reason and compassion."

For a conservative, that's an awfully bitter pill to swallow. So as I layered in my defense mechanisms, I even found myself saying things like, "If I took the time to respond to every presidential tweet, there would be little time for anything else." Given the volume and velocity of tweets from both the Trump campaign and then the White House, this was certainly true. But it was also a monumental dodge. It would be like Noah saying, "If I spent all my time obsessing about the coming flood, there would be little time for anything else." At a certain point, if one is being honest, the flood becomes the thing that is most worthy of attention. At a certain point, it might be time to build an ark.

Under our constitution, there simply are not that many people who are in a position to do something about an executive branch in chaos. As the first branch of government (Article I), the Congress was designed expressly to assert itself at just such moments. It is what we talk about when we talk about "checks and balances." Too often we observe the unfolding drama along with the rest of the country, passively, all but saying, *"Someone should do something!"* without seeming to realize that that someone is us. And so, that unnerving silence in the face of an erratic executive branch is an abdication, and those in positions of leadership bear particular responsibility.

There was a time when the leadership of the Congress from both parties felt an institutional loyalty that would frequently create bonds across party lines in defense of congressional prerogatives in a unified front against the White House, regardless of the president's party. We do not have to go very far back to identify these exemplars—the Bob Doles and Howard Bakers and Richard Lugars of the Senate. Vigorous partisans, yes, but even more importantly, principled constitutional conservatives whose primary interest was in governing and making America truly great.

But then the period of collapse and dysfunction set in, amplified by the Internet and our growing sense of alienation from each other, and we lost our way and began to rationalize away our principles in the process. But where does such capitulation take us? If by 2017 the conservative bargain was to go along for the very bumpy ride because with congressional hegemony and the White House we had the numbers to achieve some long-held policy goals—even as we put at risk our institutions and our values—then it was a very real question whether any such policy victories wouldn't be pyrrhic ones. If this was our Faustian bargain, then it was not worth it. If ultimately our principles were so malleable as to no longer be principles, then what was the point of political victories in the first place?

Meanwhile, the strange specter of an American president's seeming affection for strongmen and authoritarians created such a cognitive dissonance among my generation of conservatives—who had come of age under existential threat from the Soviet Union—that it was almost impossible to believe. Even as our own government was documenting a concerted attack against our democratic processes by an enemy foreign power, our own White House was rejecting the authority of its own intelligence agencies, disclaiming their findings as a Democratic ruse and a hoax. Conduct that would have had conservatives up in arms had it been exhibited by our political opponents now had us dumbstruck.

It was then that I was compelled back to Senator Goldwater's book, to a chapter entitled "The Soviet Menace." Since the fall of the Berlin Wall, this part of Goldwater's critique had seemed particularly anachronistic. The lesson here is that nothing is gone forever, especially when it comes to the devouring ambition of despotic men. As Goldwater wrote in that chapter:

> Our forebears knew that "keeping a Republic" meant, above all, keeping it safe from foreign transgressors; they knew that a people cannot live and work freely, and develop national institutions conducive to freedom, except in peace and with independence.

We have taken those "institutions conducive to freedom" for granted as we have engaged in one of the more reckless periods of politics in our history. By the spring of 2017, we seemed to have lost our appreciation for just how hard-won and vulnerable those institutions are.

CHAPTER SEVEN

NOTE TO SELVES: COUNTRY BEFORE PARTY

At what point then is the approach of danger to be expected?
I answer, if it ever reach us, it must spring up amongst us.
It cannot come from abroad. If destruction be our lot, we must
ourselves be its author and finisher. As a nation of freemen,
we must live through all time, or die by suicide.

—ABRAHAM LINCOLN, January 1838

No man is above the law and no man is below it; nor do we ask
any man's permission when we require him to obey it. . . .
Obedience to the law is demanded as a right; not asked as a favor.

—THEODORE ROOSEVELT, December 1903

Conservatism, we are told, is out-of-date. The charge is
preposterous and we ought boldly to say so. The laws of God,
and of nature, have no dateline. . . . These principles are derived
from the nature of man, and from the truths that God has revealed
about His creation. . . . To suggest that the Conservative philoso-
phy is out of date is akin to saying that the Golden Rule, or the
Ten Commandments or Aristotle's Politics are out of date.

—BARRY GOLDWATER, *The Conscience of a Conservative*, 1960

Freedom is never more than one generation away from extinction.
We didn't pass it to our children in the bloodstream. It must be
fought for, protected, and handed on for them to do the same.

—RONALD REAGAN, March 1961

A S A KID, for as long as I can remember, a 3x5 card, stained with vegetable oil, cookie dough, and brownie mix, was pasted on our refrigerator. It read: "Assume the best, Look for the good." To-do lists, wedding invitations, school pictures, ribbons from the county fair came and went over the years, but that card remained. "Assume the best, Look for the good" was as close to a motto as our family had. So much so that this phrase still adorns refrigerators on handwritten cards and even hangs above doorways on stenciled wood in the homes of nearly all of my parents' children.

I am so grateful to my parents for giving me that creed— "Assume the best, Look for the good"—as a prism through which to see the world. And if there is a thing under the sun I relish less than lecturing friends, I can't think of it just now. But if I didn't know better, I would say that we had not been in our right minds in the days leading up to the presidential election in 2016.

What does it say about conservatives that our message by then was so different from the words that my parents taught me, so different as to amount to a rejection of the optimistic vision of Ronald Reagan or the extraordinary decency of George H. W. Bush, or the principled constitutionalism of Barry Goldwater? What does it say that we had instead succumbed to what can only be described as a propaganda-fueled dystopian view of conservatism? And what does that, in turn, say about our stewardship of America and its institutions?

What it says is that we are as capable as anyone of forgetting our priorities, of putting politics before patriotism, and of putting party before country. Populist resentments may feel good in the moment, but indulging them is destructive, and *self-destructive*, and offers no solutions to the very real problems that gave rise to the resentments in the first place. Manipulating populist resentments is the oldest trick in the book, and it is shameful. When we allow ourselves to prioritize winning at all costs over what is best for our country, when we ignore conscience in the face of things that we know are wrong, when we reduce our rich democracy to a series of purely binary calculations, then we have chosen our political interests over the public interest, and in so doing we inflict great harm on the country. We cannot claim to place the highest premium on character, then abruptly suspend the importance of character in the most vital civic decision that we make. When we excuse on our side what we attack on the other, then we are hypocrites. If we do that as a practice, then we are corrupt. If we continually accept this conduct as elected officials, then perhaps we shouldn't *be* elected officials.

To that last point, it is important to make a distinction between those who are led and those who are leaders, between the citizens of our country—be they in Arizona, Alabama, or Alaska—who are doing their best to get by and doing their best to choose leaders from a sometimes sorry lot. To be clear: I completely understand and support the people of the United States who in great frustration and with great hope voted for Donald Trump for president. In the course of this book, I have attempted to lay bare some of the reasons I could not pull the lever. Trust me when I say that it was one of the most agonizing decisions of my political life to withhold my support for the nominee of my party. As a conservative, I try not to act impulsively with the public's business, and so sometimes I feel as if I am traversing the air over the Grand Canyon without so much as a tightrope. Nothing would make me happier than to be able to support the president wholeheartedly, and I have said many times that I will support him when I can and oppose him when

I must. In good conscience and good faith, and in pledging my best to the people of Arizona, that is all I can do.

Any president will take just about any authority he or she is given. It is the job of Congress to push back, to contain and counter the power of the president when necessary. This is not a radical statement, it is simply a matter of exercising our constitutional obligations. As the old saying goes, we've got to use it or lose it.

As distressing as the current state of our politics is, let us not forget that our institutions have seen worse than us. What saw us through those times was always the sanctuary of sound principle and a sufficient number of civic-minded countrymen who pulled us back from the brink. We have allowed ourselves to be encouraged toward the brink too much, by provocateurs and disrupters with an explicit agenda to tear down rather than build up.

Ours has been a period of insult and imputation to rival any such period in our history, and its effects will outlive us. This was a period in which we disrupted only to disrupt, destroyed only to destroy; it was a period replete with self-described Leninists (on our side) who thought it was cool to revel in the damage they could do, in the name of economic nationalism. Because we were too attentive to the politics at the expense of principle, we conservatives forgot to announce to the American people just how much we don't like Leninists. We forgot to affirm in a voice loud and clear that yes, we are proud Republicans, but that we believe in country before party. We forgot to do that. We were *afraid* to do that. We rationalized that failure in a hundred ways—"Oh, that's just shock and awe politics." It's just tactical, we told ourselves. Many of us even admired its hubris, even as we seemed oblivious to the moral injury that it caused us all.

Earlier generations would likely have known what to do had they faced what we faced in the second decade of the twenty-first century. In fact, our current crisis is precisely why Madison, Hamilton, and Jay went through the painstaking public deliberation that would give us the United States Constitution, leaving us their record of it in the Federalist Papers, a towering collection of essays that argued that crucial document into existence. Citizens of all stripes can find much wisdom in those pages, especially in a time of such severe testing for our institutions.

When the behavior of a White House is defined by fixed habits and flexible principles, then the coequal branches of our government must not defer, defend, or deflect. In the case of the Congress, we must always protect the institution we have been elected to lead.

Federalist No. 51 is a miracle of clear reason on the subject of our separation of powers, and it rewards repeated readings. It was of course written before we had split ourselves into parties—February 1788—before the fall, you might say, when Americans knew who and what the real enemies of liberty were and were united in a purpose that would soon enough give way to a factionalism that has hardly ceased since. But given the degree to which we have now divided ourselves, we would do well to look to the architects of our freedom for guidance.

If ever we fall into thinking that our present dilemmas have never been foreseen or forewarned, this is owed only to our lack of reading, because the Founders, of course, anticipated our contemporary worries wonderfully. Written by James Madison (as "Publius"), Federalist No. 51 is known for its theme, which aptly describes the problem of human nature that it proposed to solve: "The Safety of Multiple Interests: Ambition Will Counteract Ambition."

Allow me to quote a passage or two:

To what expedient, then, shall we finally resort, for maintaining in practice the necessary partition of power among the several departments, as laid down in the Constitution? The only answer that can be given is . . . by so contriving the interior structure of the government as that its several constituent parts may, by their mutual relations, be the means of keeping each other in their proper places.

. . . the great security against a gradual concentration of the several powers in the same department, consists in giving to those who administer each department the necessary constitutional means and personal motives to resist encroachments of the others. The provision for defense must in this, as in all other cases, be made commensurate to the danger of attack. Ambition must be made to counteract ambition. . . . It may be a reflection on human nature, that such devices should be necessary to control the abuses of government. But what is government itself, but the greatest of all reflections on human nature? If men were angels, no government would be necessary. If angels were to govern men, neither external nor internal controls on government would be necessary. In framing a government which is to be administered by men over men, the great difficulty lies in this: you must first enable the government to control the governed; and in the next place oblige it to control itself. . . .

Madison makes clear his intention that "in republican government, the legislative authority necessarily predominates," by which he meant that the members of Congress stand for election just as the president does, and they serve at the pleasure of no one but the people from whom their authority is derived. Coming out of a century in which the presidency has taken on unforeseen and unequal powers, from one party to the next and in a creeping fashion, returning to what the Founders themselves said on the subject is the best remedy of all.

Servile partisanship can cause you to act in ways that you

might not otherwise act. In our time, misplaced loyalty has caused some conservative members of Congress to declare that they serve at the pleasure of the president, which Mr. Madison would have found quite surprising. A Republican president named Roosevelt had just the idea for putting a president in his place:

> The President is merely the most important among a large number of public servants. He should be supported or opposed exactly to the degree which is warranted by his good conduct or bad conduct, his efficiency or inefficiency in rendering loyal, able, and disinterested service to the Nation as a whole. Therefore it is absolutely necessary that there should be full liberty to tell the truth about his acts, and this means that it is exactly as necessary to blame him when he does wrong as to praise him when he does right. Any other attitude in an American citizen is both base and servile. To announce that there must be no criticism of the President, or that we are to stand by the President, right or wrong, is not only unpatriotic and servile, but is morally treasonable to the American public.

Teddy Roosevelt wrote those words while the United States was embroiled in World War I, in case anyone thinks that even a wartime president is immune to criticism. Roosevelt knew that paying obeisance to power—regardless of how well intentioned—is a danger to our balance of powers and the opposite of conservatism.

In a time of institutional uncertainty, if the proper checks and balances are to be preserved, we must act on conscience and principle. The Senate must be the saucer that cools the coffee, as George Washington is said to have told Thomas Jefferson. A case in point early in the new presidency was President Trump's increasing pressure on the Senate to dispense with the filibuster for legislation so that he might be able to get his program through the Senate without concern about achieving consensus. Such a move would turn the Senate into just another majoritarian body just like the House of Representatives, thus forfeiting its reputation as a deliberative body at all, much less the world's greatest. At that point, it might be fair to ask: Why have a Senate at all? Legislating is supposed to be hard. The legislative filibuster protects the rights of the minority and forces compromise. Wiser men than we dreamed it up for just that purpose. We won't always be in the majority and so would surely live to regret such a move, for practical reasons if for nothing else. Dealmaking would be less of a negotiation and more of a declaration. *I win. You lose.*

That is not how constitutional democracy works. And it's not how the United States Senate works, either.

How willing would the Republicans be to go along with the president? Would we be willing to change the institution for short-term gain? We all consider ourselves institutionalists, but what will we do when the president starts tweeting, scolding us for obstructing his agenda? What happens if there is a tax bill which isn't getting any Democratic support, will we stand up and say no, we've got to be bipartisan, we've got to work for it and pick up the necessary votes? Or will we scrap the rules?

I will not support any such effort to harm the Senate. It is a line I cannot cross. Assuming all forty-eight Democrats would also oppose any such effort, if just three Republicans join them, we could block it. There would, no doubt, be consequences. But so, too, would there be consequences if we were not to act.

Acting on conscience and principle is the manner in which we express our moral selves, and as such, loyalty to conscience and principle should supersede loyalty to any man or party. We can all be forgiven for failing in that measure from time to time. As I have written, I certainly put myself at the top of the list of those who fall short in that regard. I am holier-than-none. But too often, we rush not to salvage principle but to forgive and excuse our failures and the failures of our partisans, maybe even deny them, so that we might accommodate them and go right on failing—until the accommodation itself becomes our principle.

In that way and over time, we can justify almost any behavior and sacrifice almost any principle. That is where we now find ourselves, I am afraid. I ask myself: To whom are we loyal? And what behavior in ourselves will we defend or ignore, that we would never countenance in our opponents? And to what end?

The conservative writer Charlie Sykes has written about how the "safe space" for conservatives is no longer adhering to conservative principle but rather trolling liberals—he dubbed this "anti-anti-Trumpism," a form of conservatism that exists not to do good or advance ideas but only to feast on the indignation of its opponents. Sykes correctly said that this was a form of conservatism that Goldwater would not have recognized. Neither do I.

We came to a fork in the road back there somewhere, and we went the wrong way. We took the road too often traveled—of venality and mendacity and political expediency. We have gone farther and faster down that road than anyone has before. It is now time to take the road less traveled. It is a harder path, but we will be better for its difficulty.

We must be willing to risk our careers to save our principles. That is certainly what those four men whose quotes begin this chapter would have done. Incidentally, lest it be doubted that this is a time like no other, the question often arises whether those Republican exemplars would today even be welcomed in our party. Consider that for a moment, in case you suppose that there is anything normal about the political era we have entered.

The worn refrigerator card I grew up with didn't read "Assume the worst, and pick sides." It read, and still reads: "Assume the best, Look for the good." I'll take my chances with the goodness and wisdom of my parents. We have tried the other way and have made a hash of things. When all else has failed, let us do the right thing.

My father is old now. It's been some time since he embarked, as Ronald Reagan put it, into the sunset of his life. As his mind slowly softens and takes him away, he'll sometimes look at my mother, with whom through his faith he knows he will spend eternity, and say, "I'm not going anywhere, you're stuck with me," and laugh. My father, whose body bears the scars left by unbroken horses, untamed bulls, and unforgiving farm equipment, still has a strength of character to which I can only aspire. In all my time emulating him, I have never known him to have a moment's malice for anyone. Could a son have a better example for life? I honestly don't think so.

Conservative? You bet. And supremely decent. Those things are not mutually exclusive.

One evening not long ago, a dozen or so members of our family gathered in my parents' living room in Snowflake, and the talk ranged from the playful banter brothers engage in to the tempestuous politics of the day. Dad sat on the edge of the conversation, listening quietly. Since his mind had begun to slip, he doesn't join in much anymore. But then he said something rather remarkable. The room was pretty raucous, and Dad's voice is rather soft, but the room got quiet, and we all turned to look his way. "What you need to do is listen to everybody," he said. "A little patience. Then you get everybody going in the same direction, that's how it works best."

"Exactly right, Dad," I said.

It was my father who taught me what I know about putting country before party. He is teaching me still.

CHAPTER EIGHT

DEAR WORLD: BEAR WITH US

Oh, it's home again, and home again, America for me!
I want a ship that's westward bound to plough the rolling sea,
To the blessed Land of Room Enough beyond the ocean bars,
Where the air is full of sunlight and the flag is full of stars

—HENRY VAN DYKE, 1909

I RECEIVED ONE OF MY MOST VALUABLE LESSONS in democracy when I was a young man, far from home. I was sitting in the capital of a new African democracy, reading a speech by the leader of a new European democracy that invoked Abraham Lincoln's "Family of Man" speech, when it struck me just how vital a beacon the United States is to the peoples of the world—both to those who are already free and to those who suffer tyranny. Almost thirty years later, I struggle to adequately convey the power of that moment and that reminder.

For my church mission, I went to South Africa, learned Afrikaans and a passable amount of various tribal dialects, and generally fell in love with the people of that country. Drawn back to southern Africa a few years later for a job, I was in Windhoek, Namibia, in February of 1990, at the very moment that much of the world enslaved by totalitarianism was throwing off its shackles, and the "free world" that the United States had lead since World War II was growing exponentially. The Soviet Union was in a glorious free fall, shedding republics seemingly by the day, and Eastern Europe was squinting out into the light of liberation for the first time in forty years. Free markets and free minds were sweeping the world.

Freedom was breaking out in the Southern Hemisphere as well. The country where I was sitting that morning was itself only days old. In November 1989, the same week the Berlin Wall fell, Namibia had held its first election as an independent nation, freed from the apartheid administration of South Africa. This came to pass without a shot fired and in no small part because of leadership from the United States, through the United Nations. Just days earlier, an awe-inspiring document had been drafted only blocks away from where I sat in Windhoek—a new democracy's founding constitution, the inspiration for which had been the marvel of free people everywhere and those who aspire to be free, the United States Constitution.

At the time, I was in Africa working for the Foundation for Democracy, trying to ensure that Namibia emerged from the process of gaining its independence as a democratic country. In my role at the foundation, I evangelized for democracy and democratic values, the benefits of which had been a given for me for my entire life. I can safely say, though, that I learned more about democracy from the lives of those around me who aspired to it rather than those who experienced it as a birthright.

As I sat there in the brand-new African democracy, I read the speech that the playwright and new president of a newly democratic Czechoslovakia, Vaclav Havel, had just delivered before a joint session of the United States Congress. Havel, who had spent much of the previous decade in a communist dungeon and whose last arrest as a dissident had been a mere four months before, was astonished to find himself president of anything, much less the country of his oppressors. I sat and read Havel's speech—an encomium to democracy, a love letter to America, literary and inspiring—and I was overcome by his words. There is nothing quite like the sensation of having a man who has been stripped of everything but his dignity reflecting the ideals of your own country back at you, in such a way that you see them more clearly than ever before. In some ways, that man knows your country better than you do. Perhaps most humbling was that Havel could never have known that his fidelity to the universal truths contained in our founding documents could ever have resulted in anything but his misery and imprisonment, maybe even his death. And yet, from the darkness of his deprivation, he had faith. His life depended on that faith.

I can now only imagine the surreality Havel felt as he stood before the entire Congress, the president's cabinet, the diplomatic corps, and the Joint Chiefs of Staff assembled before him in the House chamber in our Capitol Building, with the vice president and the Speaker of the House behind him, all standing in a sustained ovation, a deep show of respect from the oldest democracy on earth to the newest, whose leader had been a political prisoner just a season earlier. Havel soberly poured out his gratitude to the United States for the sacrifices that our country had made in liberating Europe once again and for the moral example of its leadership around the world in opposing the Soviet Union, "the country that rightly gave people nightmares."

He spoke in Czech to a riveted audience but made a point to transition to English to say this: "When Thomas Jefferson wrote that 'governments are instituted among men, deriving their just powers from the consent of the governed,' it was a simple and important act of the human spirit. What gave meaning to that act, however, was the fact that the author backed it up with his life. It was not just his words; it was his deed as well."

Spoken by a man from a country where only weeks before there had been no such thing as "just power" or "the consent of the governed," Havel's awed appreciation for the values that too many of us might take for granted bought home to me, an American in my late twenties sitting there in Africa, the power of the American example to the whole world. And the humbling responsibilities that come with that power.

It is no exaggeration to say that Havel's disquisition on democracy before Congress that day in 1990 was a turning point in my life, and certainly in my civic education, as it took the new president of Czechoslovakia to enlighten a kid from Arizona about a speech that Abraham Lincoln had given in 1858, as he contemplated running for president, a speech in which Lincoln spoke of the "Family of Man."

"These revolutionary changes," Havel said, "will enable us to escape from the rather antiquated straitjacket of this bipolar view of the world and to enter at last into an era of multipolarity, that is, into an era in which all of us, large and small, former slaves and former masters, will be able to create what your great President Lincoln called 'the family of man.'"

I had to find out what Havel was talking about. Of course, being in a developing nation, there were few computers and there was no Internet just yet, and a copy of Lincoln's speech would prove hard to get, but it was worth the search. Lincoln knew that democracy and self-determination were neither permanent nor inevitable, and he was calling out to the whole world as he drew on the wisdom of his forebears and mustered his energies for the bloody struggle for American democracy that was to come:

These communities, by their representatives in old Independence Hall, said to the whole world of men: "We hold these truths to be self evident: that all men are created equal; that they are endowed by their Creator with certain unalienable rights; that among these are life, liberty and the pursuit of happiness." This was their majestic interpretation of the economy of the Universe. This was their lofty, and wise, and noble understanding of the justice of the Creator to His creatures. Yes, gentlemen, to *all* His creatures, to the whole great family of man. In their enlightened belief, nothing stamped with the Divine image and likeness was sent into the world to be trodden on, and degraded, and imbruted by its fellows. They grasped not only the whole race of man then living, but they reached forward and seized upon the farthest posterity. They erected a beacon to guide their children and their children's children, and the countless myriads who should inhabit the earth in other ages. Wise statesmen as they were, they knew the tendency of prosperity to breed tyrants, and so they established these great self-evident truths, that when in the distant future some man, some faction, some interest, should set up the doctrine that none but rich men, or none but white men, were entitled to life, liberty and the pursuit of happiness, their posterity might look up again to the Declaration of Independence and take courage to renew the battle which their fathers began—so that truth, and justice, and mercy, and all the humane and Christian virtues might not be extinguished from the land; so that no man would hereafter dare to limit and circumscribe the great principles on which the temple of liberty was being built.

Lincoln might have been speaking to a small gathering in Illinois, but his was a text both ancient and a century before its time, and for my personal experience of it I had a short avant-garde Czech playwright to thank. Havel similarly called out to the whole world from Washington that day in early 1990, with grace and without rancor, in a speech that deserves to live as long as Lincoln's, but for one mistaken prophecy, that to me now reads as tragic. At the time, as the wall fell and the Soviet bloc that had been encased in Stalinism thawed, it was a vogue among some historians, scholars, and others to declare "the end of history"—that the big questions had been settled, that liberal democracy was triumphal and inexorable, and that the decline of the blackhearted impulse to enslave whole countries was also inexorable. Freedom had won, it was said, and for ever. The historian Francis Fukuyama, who had coined "the end of history" in an essay the year before, was much in demand, and it is likely that Havel would have been inspired by the fervor, which would explain this passage from his speech: "I often hear the question: How can the United States of America help us today? My reply is as paradoxical as the whole of my life has been. You can help us most of all if you help the Soviet Union on its irreversible but immensely complicated road to democracy."

Of course, history was not over, and the road to democracy is not irreversible—not in Moscow, not in America, not anywhere. After erecting a Potemkin village of democracy for an agonizing decade or so, the Russians thrust forward a strongman amid the chaos, a strongman who was determined to reassemble the pieces of broken empire, in the process strangling Russian democracy in its cradle. Vladimir Putin would go on to be president and is president still, and just as he disrupted democracy in his own country, he is determined to do so everywhere.

This is something that is staring us in the face, right now, as I write this. As we in America contemplate the hard-won conventions and norms of democracy, trust me when I tell you that we realize that none of this is permanent and that it must be fought for constantly. Civilization and the victories of freedom—history itself—are not a matter of once achieved, always safe. Vaclav Havel lived this. The lovers of democracy I

met in Namibia lived this. Our children, whose rights and prerogatives have never for a moment been in doubt, are for the
most part unaware of it. But we are being powerfully reminded
just how delicate all of this is—right now.

The stability of tested alliances, the steadiness of comportment, and the consistency of words and deeds sum up the best
of water's-edge postwar American consensus on foreign policy
and address to the world. I know it might seem that all of this
has lately been tossed around like pieces on a board, which,
obviously, sometimes has the world on edge, but just know that
we have seen tumult and trial before, and it is the genius of the
architects of our liberty that we withstand it all and emerge
stronger for it. America is and will be America, even as the Russian empire strikes back and strongmen persist and the durability of the very idea of constitutional democracy is tested, in my
own country and the world over. Please don't think that the
United States is indifferent to any of this.

One of our greatest leaders imagined a world that he never
saw and described the "family of man" so powerfully that he lit
a torch bright enough to be seen in all corners of the globe, in
apartheid Africa and the communist dungeons of Cold War
Europe, in Syrian refugee camps, in authoritarian regimes, and
in oppressive theocracies. Just as America will never give up on
you, I know that you will never give up on America.

CHAPTER NINE

TOWARD A NEW CONSERVATISM

I'm convinced that today the majority of Americans want what those first Americans wanted: A better life for themselves and their children; a minimum of government authority. Very simply, they want to be left alone in peace and safety to take care of the family by earning an honest dollar and putting away some savings. This may not sound too exciting, but there is something magnificent about it. On the farm, on the street corner, in the factory and in the kitchen, millions of us ask nothing more, but certainly nothing less than to live our own lives according to our values—at peace with ourselves, our neighbors and the world.

—RONALD REAGAN, July 6, 1976

WHEN I WAS GROWING UP on a ranch in northern Arizona, one of my more unusual chores was a job I called "bloat watch." I would sit atop a hill with knife in hand, watching cattle grazing on the green alfalfa field below. The cows would sometimes eat too much too fast, and their gluttony could be lethal. As soon as the first cow assumed the bloated position (on its side, with four feet sticking straight out) I would rush to the victim, raise the knife, and stab just behind the last rib high on the left side, to relieve the pressure. I would then try to take cover as pent-up gas and alfalfa spewed upward, ultimately raining down around me. I'm sure that being stabbed wasn't pleasant for the cow, but the alternative was fatal.

After I was elected to Congress in 2000 and saw our bloated spending bills, I sometimes wished I'd kept my old knife.

The most offensive type of spending, which was exploding in the late 1990s and early 2000s, was "earmarking," the practice of quietly inserting parochial spending items deep within large appropriation bills. While bipartisanship was waning in other areas in Congress, it was alive and well when it came to earmarking. I immediately set my sights on trying to end this type of spending by proposing amendments to strip out earmarks when spending bills came to the House floor for a vote.

My opposition to earmarks was not so much because of the value of the earmarks alone. I opposed them mostly because to protect their earmarks, members of Congress—liberals and conservatives alike—would vote for grotesquely bloated appropriations bills that they otherwise might not have supported, just to protect their cherished pork. What's more, there began to be a strong correlation between earmarks going out and campaign contributions coming in. The concept of "pay-to-play" became so pervasive that something urgently needed to be done.

Either a "principled approach" or "a strong showing of stupidity." That's how one of my Republican colleagues once described my offering thirty-one amendments on the House floor to strip funding for earmarks.

Offering amendments to strike earmarks became a regular practice for me, and while that practice won me no popularity contests, I enjoyed it immensely. It was a lonely endeavor, but I did receive the quiet support of the House parliamentarian, who seemed as worried as I was about the integrity of the institution. The parliamentarian's office tutored me in how to create amendments that couldn't be blocked by members of the leadership.

Before offering my first-ever anti-earmark amendments, I called Senator Tom Coburn of Oklahoma, who while in the House had once singlehandedly stopped a bill in its tracks by offering such an onslaught of amendments that the committee was forced to pull the bill just to stop the carnage. We would later refer to that move as the "Coburn filibuster," and I would use the tactic a time or two myself.

But until I decided to do it, nobody had tried to block funding for a series of earmarks on the House floor. I asked Coburn if he had any advice. He said "Be prepared to get yelled at, ridiculed, jeered and threatened, because you'll get it all." He added: "But don't worry, in the end they'll respect you."

Well, Coburn was at least right about the first part.

These fights definitely had me tilting at windmills, and sometimes even at the Speaker of the House of my own party. My habit was to release a list of earmarks I would challenge, and one evening I got a call from a reporter asking if I knew that I was challenging one of Speaker Hastert's earmarks. I didn't, but I wasn't at all surprised. The reporter asked if I would still offer the amendment. I told him I would.

The issue was particularly sensitive because a story had just been published reporting that Speaker Hastert had bought a piece of property in rural Illinois in 2004, secured a $200 million earmark for a nearby highway and interchange in 2005, then sold the property for a $2 million profit that same year.

I offered my amendment targeting Speaker Hastert's earmark, and the Speaker dispatched Ray LaHood, his fellow Illinoisan, to defend the $2.5 million he had slipped into the defense bill, which went to an organization called the Illinois Technology Transition Center, which had been established by one of Hastert's former staffers.

The transcript of my exchange with Congressman LaHood goes as follows:

> MR. LaHOOD: Mr. Chairman, I ask to have the opportunity to speak against the amendment. I wonder if the gentleman would take a question.
> MR. FLAKE: You bet.
> MR. LaHOOD: Do you know who earmarked this money?
> MR. FLAKE: I was told by a reporter this morning who it might be.
> MR. LaHOOD: And the answer to my question is?
> MR. FLAKE: I was told that it was the Speaker who offered it.
> MR. LaHOOD: And so when you were told that, did you think that maybe you might look into the earmark to see if it had merit and to see if it was a set-aside that might merit further consideration?
> MR. FLAKE: Well, seeing that I had already agreed to offer it, I thought that had I agreed to pull back now, I would be looked to favoring one particularly powerful member of my party.

I'm not exactly sure what Ray LaHood, or the Speaker, wanted to accomplish with that exchange. Were they trying to get me to withdraw the amendment at that stage in the game? Didn't they realize that it would be far worse for the Speaker if I had withdrawn the amendment under pressure? A decade later, I'm still scratching my head on that one. In any event, my amendment failed by a voice vote.

The next morning, *The Hill* carried the front page headline "Flake Strikes at Earmark of Hastert's." The article noted that "the amendment, one of about 10 he offered, was expected to fail miserably as of press time." They got that right. But I wasn't wrong. I lost that battle and many more after that. But we won the war. Soon, members of Congress whose earmarks I planned to challenge began to rush to the floor to withdraw the earmarks rather than defend them. In 2009 both the House and Senate banned the practice of earmarking.

Perhaps because I was naive, it never occurred to me to not do what I thought was right just because my opponent in that instance was a member of my own party, not to mention the most powerful member of the House of Representatives.

Perhaps we should endeavor to remain so naive. Because when we are at our best, we *govern*. We do not fear to challenge our own party or work with those on the other side of the aisle. We are resolute in our principle and flexible in our partisanship. We assume the best and look for the good. These things are what the people have the right to expect from us, and they also double as the best practices.

There is no gimmick, no shortcut, no ten-point plan, no magic in what must come to make our movement and our politics healthy again. The values that will redeem us are ancient and the road ahead is difficult, which is as it should be, because we know as conservatives that nothing that lasts and is worthwhile comes easily or quickly.

During 2013, my first year in the Senate, I became part of a bipartisan group—led by the senior senator from Arizona, John McCain—that was set on dealing with America's long-neglected need for comprehensive immigration reform. Bipartisan groups in Congress are almost always called "gangs," as if bipartisanship is some kind of outlaw activity, but in any case the group became known as the "Gang of Eight." And the bill that we would produce was one of the few major bills in years to be produced under what is known as "regular order."

Regular order means that the House and the Senate run according to the standing rules of both bodies and that the twelve appropriations bills that we are required to pass are passed on time—at the time of this writing, this has not happened in twenty years. Regular order means that standing committees are charged with producing good legislation after thorough hearings. It means that the members of the House—whether in the majority or minority—are allowed to offer amendments to legislation. It means that the House and the Senate convene in formal conferences to reconcile legislation. It means that the Congress pays for emergency spending requests and doesn't put major spending items on a credit card.

And regular order also means that both parties in a "gang" engage in the sometimes excruciating work of arguing and compromise. This was part of the reason I wanted to go to the Senate—because its institutional strictures require you to cross the aisle and do what is best for the country. That is both the hindrance and the benefit of the filibuster. It is rare that one party ever has sixty votes, and so rather than one side dictatorially pressing its partisan advantage and producing fatally flawed laws, the rules of the Senate force us to govern, and to be adults, whether we like it or not. Because what is best for the country is for neither base to fully get what it wants but rather for the factions that make up our parties to be compelled to talk until we find policy solutions to our problems. To listen to the rhetoric of the extremes of both parties, one could be forgiven for believing that we are each other's enemies, that we are at war with ourselves.

Hyper-partisans both create and benefit most from this perception and are probably the greatest impediments to real progress, because they thrive in an atmosphere of dysfunction. When the politics is frozen by suspicion, bad faith, and ill will, the hyper-partisan is free to criticize, without the nettlesome obligation of having to actually work to accomplish something. Hyper-partisans believe that the only acceptable outcome is for them to get precisely what they want, which betrays a basic misunderstanding of governance, not to mention the realities of life as an adult.

The Gang of Eight—four Republicans, four Democrats— proved that the process as designed can actually work. We would meet for seven months of tough and tense negotiations, and produce a comprehensive bill on immigration that would address the problem for the first time in a generation. Weighing in at more than a thousand pages, the bill was a good result of a good process—far from perfect but rigorous and honest, a bill that sought to fix our immigration problems and addressed the concerns of both sides. And when the bill passed committee and made it to the floor, both Republicans and Democratic members of the Gang of Eight worked to protect the integrity of the compromise bill, beating back amendments that they might otherwise have been inclined to support. Republicans were in the minority in the Senate at the time, but it's worth remembering that my fellow Republican Senators Grassley and Cornyn—who opposed the bill—made a point of saying that they did not block its consideration on the floor because they felt they had received a fair hearing in committee. That is an example of the process as it should work.

More recently, early in 2017 Senator Tim Kaine and I began work on a bill to give authorization for the president to use military force against ISIS, al-Qaeda, and the Taliban. Call it a Gang of Two. The country had been functioning under the sixteen-year-old AUMF (authorization for use of military force) that authorized military force against al-Qaeda in Afghanistan after 9/11, and it was high time for the Congress to assert itself and fulfill its constitutional obligations on the subject of war and peace. The fact that we hadn't was, frankly, shameful. Another abdication, in an era of abdication.

Senator Kaine and I started talking about the bill not long after President Obama drew his infamous red line in Syria in 2013. After the despot Bashar al-Assad crossed that line by using chemical weapons against his own people, Obama, seemingly cowed by intense domestic opposition to involving the United States in yet another Middle Eastern conflict, took no military action at all. Instead, the president dispatched his secretary of state, John Kerry, to ask Congress for authorization to retaliate for the heinous attack on civilians.

Appearing before the Senate Foreign Relations Committee, Secretary Kerry gave me a scolding for having the temerity to ask why he was coming to us for permission to enforce a red line that the president himself had drawn. He said, in so many words, that it was surprising that a senator would begrudge an administration coming to the Senate for authority to do this. I questioned whether we had lost a strategic advantage by waiting, because surely Assad would move his chemical weapons in the interim. The White House could have followed through on its well-advertised pledge to rein in Assad and then come to Congress to inform us on what the administration planned to do going forward. If there was imminent danger, the White House ought not use Congress as an excuse not to act.

The president blinked, but the Congress had long since gone blind. The Constitution gives only the Congress the ability to declare war, and the United States has not declared war since December 11, 1941, with the formal declaration against Germany and Italy (we went to war against Japan on December 8). And so the Congress has been slowly ceding its Article I powers to the White House for the better part of a century and has largely been a bystander to some very consequential unilateral commitments of military force undertaken by presidents in this century.

Before any talk of red lines, Senator Kaine and I and other members of the committee had met in the Roosevelt Room at the White House with President Obama's national security staff. The White House was interested in asking Congress for a new AUMF, and wanted to explore how to go about doing so. This was a vital conversation for us to be having, as the threats had grown and fragmented, and as the new threat landscape involved almost entirely non-state actors, such as the "Islamic State." What authorities did the White House need? Did Congress need to repeal the 2001 AUMF? Before we could answer those questions, politics intervened once again, and Congress once again failed to act.

So it was with a renewed sense of purpose in the first few months of the Trump presidency that Senator Kaine and I drafted legislation to expressly give the president authority to act on the current threats that we face. The law would expire after five years so that Congress could reassess that authority, and should the threat environment change in the meantime, the president would be required to come to Congress to ask for new authority. The bill earned headlines such as "Senators Make New Push to Rein in Trump's Military Powers," which tells only half the story. I would have pushed to rein in the military powers of any occupant of the White House.

The foreign policy and treaty powers constitute an important advantage the Senate has over the House. And a six-year term allows senators to see over the next hill, to achieve consensus, to outlast an administration, and to not always be obliged to respond to the politics of the moment. Too often, it is the politics of the moment that divides the parties, stifles Congress from fulfilling its constitutional role, and baffles the country.

I am very proud of the Gang of Eight immigration bill (even though it failed in the House after passing the Senate with overwhelming bipartisan support) and the bipartisan war powers bill. That is the way the system once worked and is how it has worked when we are at our best. But if those might be considered examples of how the legislative process works when it works best, there are many more examples of the system at its abysmal worst.

For instance, just because the deliberations over Obamacare in 2009 were a thoroughly partisan affair—and they were—does not mean that Republicans should compound the mistake by planning its repeal behind closed doors. Legislation executed without hearings and written by only one side is always a bad idea, regardless of who does it. It is, simply put, no way to do important work. The resulting policy will almost certainly be met with rage by half the country. Rancorous partisans could spend all of their time reversing the other side's results every two years until the cows come home. By carrying on this way, we disgrace ourselves and fail the country.

Similarly, President Obama's Iran nuclear deal was far too important a matter to be a strictly partisan affair. It should obviously have been submitted to the Senate as a treaty. I told the president so. Yes, there was opposition to the Obama presidency that was irrational and intransigent—just as there was to the Bush presidency before him—but that is no justification for abandoning the constitutional guidance on how significant international agreements are to be done. Had the White House come to the Congress and made a persuasive case that Tehran was only months away from having enough enriched uranium for a nuclear device, with detailed intelligence establishing the urgency of the situation, I am confident that enough Republicans would have helped forge a binding treaty to represent the resolve of a united country. Instead, the White House bypassed the Congress altogether to create a non-binding framework that is vulnerable to being canceled by any future presidents.

An astonishing confirmation of this vulnerability came when—as the Obama White House was going around the Congress in its negotiations with Iran—forty-seven of my Republican colleagues in the Senate signed a letter addressed to the mullahs who govern Iran, essentially informing them that their negotiations with our president were invalid.

I joined a small minority of my Republican conference in not signing that letter. While I understood the impulse, I strongly disagreed with the tactic. When a group of senators is communicating directly with the leadership of a hostile foreign power, our system is sending an urgent distress signal. It is difficult to fully grasp the level of dysfunction that got us to that point. And we should all be humbled for our role in the collective failure.

It is that miasma that brought on the anomalous presidency of Donald Trump and a political era in which our democratic norms are flouted and the durability of our institutions is tested as severely as ever before. This anomalous presidency is the best argument yet for believing in those institutions, buttressing them, and defending them.

Barry Goldwater began *The Conscience of a Conservative* by writing, "This book is not written with the idea of adding to or improving on the Conservative philosophy. Or of 'bringing it up to date.' The ancient and tested truths that guided our Republic through its early days will do equally well for us. The challenge to Conservatives today is quite simply to demonstrate the bearing of a proven philosophy on the problems of our own time."

And so it is right and proper that Goldwater's beginning is where this book ends. When populism runs into realism, when disruption runs into democracy, when indecency runs into decency, we are at long last left with little choice but to once again seek refuge in principle, resort to the truth, and return to the conservatism that has been the stabilizing ballast of our republic since its founding. The alternative—which is no alternative at all—is to become further unmoored from principle and reality, to give in to our worst impulses, to fight every fight no matter how petty, to further erode trust and destroy discourse, and to continue headlong into ruin.

We must turn away from that course and prove ourselves worthy inheritors of America.

In his masterpiece *The Four Quartets,* the great American poet (and conservative) T. S. Eliot wrote: "We shall not cease from exploration / And the end of all our exploring / Will be to arrive where we started / And know the place for the first time."

In just such a way, we must, for the good of the country we love, return to the conservatism of our best traditions as if for the first time. If this is a call for a new conservatism—and it is—then it is just as well a call for the old conservatism, too. There is nothing deficient in the values that made us conservatives in the first place and that made America a freedom-loving, free-speaking conservative country—they are time-honored values. The deficiency comes in us. We have been the problem. The historians will sort out what exactly happened in this interregnum—this lapse of principle, this period of drift—they will name it, and we will learn from it many valuable lessons. And with hard work, good faith with those from whom we derive our inspiration and our authority, and maybe a little luck, we will right this ship. Not with something new and novel but with something ancient and stolid. Conservatives know that as Americans we are loyal to no man but rather to the principles of our founding.

We must embrace a conservatism that recognizes once again that our enemies are not other Americans. There is a place for robust partisanship, but with good judgment we must once again find its limits.

We must recognize that government and the process by which we go about electing our leaders ought never be confused for entertainment or graded for its entertainment value or its ratings. We degrade our politics enough as it is without turning our democracy over to carnival barkers and reality television.

We must speak the language of freedom again, not because it is a necessary sidebar to our more important activities but because it is the most important thing we can do for ourselves and for the world.

We must reaffirm our devotion once again to the rule of law.

We must embrace independence, a conservatism that calls it like it sees it, with devotion to nothing but the truth.

We must once again stand unambiguously against oppressive authoritarian regimes around the world, no matter where.

We must reject the politics of the nasty, the punitive, and the fact-free, of character assault and conspiracy, and reassert a conservatism of high ideals, goodwill, and even better arguments.

During the constitutional convention in 1787, George Washington counseled: "If, to please the people, we offer what we ourselves disprove, how can we afterwards defend our work?" It might be comfortable in an election year to warm ourselves by the populist fire that we ourselves have stoked, but it is not leadership.

Leaders appeal to the better angels of our nature rather than bow to the manifestations of our baser instincts. The standard bearer of the modern conservative movement, Ronald Reagan, understood both conservative principle and the mantle of leadership. In his farewell address in 1989 he explained:

> I've spoken of the shining city all my political life, but I don't know if I ever quite communicated what I saw when I said it. But in my mind it was a tall proud city built on rocks stronger than oceans, wind-swept, God-blessed, and teeming with people of all kinds living in harmony and peace, a city with free ports that hummed with commerce and creativity, and if there had to be city walls, the walls had doors and the doors were open to anyone with the will and the heart to get here. That's how I saw it and see it still.

This is the conscience of a conservative.

This is a rejection of destructive politics, and a return to principle.

This is not an act of apostasy. This is an act of fidelity.

ACKNOWLEDGMENTS

First and foremost, I would like to thank my wife, Cheryl, and my five children for their assistance, patience, and love as I struggled to transfer these thoughts to paper. To my ten siblings, my in-laws, and my large extended family (who usually provide the necessary margin around election time), thank you for your love, support, and good humor. And to my parents, Dean and Nerita, whose loving admonition to look for the good and assume the best motivates and inspires me every day: thank you.

Just as we were finishing this book, on June 26, 2017, my father died at his home in Snowflake—as my sister Laraine wrote beautifully in his obituary, ". . . with the windows open, a breeze blowing, the clouds building and the promise of a good rainstorm on the way."

Thank-you as well to Barry Goldwater, who launched the modern conservative movement and to whom this book is a personal homage, and to those at the Goldwater Institute, folks like Norm McClelland, Michael Block, John Norton, Barbara

Barrett, Tim Day, Roy Miller, Bob Robb, Steve Twist, among so many others, who introduced me to the writings of conservative thinkers who articulated the principles I was taught at home. And to Barry Goldwater, Jr., thank you for your suggestions and encouragement.

To my agent, David Granger, along with Andy Ward and the good folks at Random House who agreed that this book should be written and believed that this novice could write it. Thank you for lending much needed expertise and guidance.

Finally, I would like to express my deep gratitude to the people of Arizona, for giving me the honor of representing them in the United States Senate. And reaching back generations, I am indebted to those hearty souls, many of whom are my ancestors, who came to Arizona more than a century ago, before there were resorts and amenities like air-conditioning, who raised cattle and kids, built lives and communities, and showed future generations how to provide public service and govern with collegiality, consensus, and compromise.

BIBLIOGRAPHY

Founders Online (founders.archives.gov)
Inside Gov (insidegov.com)
The Laffer Center (laffercenter.com)

Bailyn, Bernard, editor. *The Debate on the Constitution.* Parts One and Two. The Library of America, 1993.

Bernanke, Ben S. *The Courage to Act: A Memoir of a Crisis and Its Aftermath.* W. W. Norton & Company, 2015.

Buckley, William F. "Goldwater, the John Birch Society, and Me." *Commentary,* March 1, 2008.

Fehrenbacher, Don E., editor. *Lincoln: Selected Speeches and Writings.* Vintage Books/The Library of America, 1992.

Flake, Osmer D. *William Jordan Flake: Pioneer, Colonizer.* Brigham Young University Press, 2000.

Goldwater, Barry. *The Conscience of a Conservative.* Victor Publishing Company, 1960.

Hayek, F. A. *The Constitution of Liberty.* The University of Chicago Press, 2011.

———. *The Fatal Conceit: The Errors of Socialism.* The University of Chicago Press, 1991.

————. *The Road to Serfdom*. The University of Chicago Press, 2007.

Hutner, Gordon. *Selected Speeches and Writings of Theodore Roosevelt*. Vintage Books, 2014.

Judis, John B. *The Populist Explosion*. Columbia Global Reports, 2016.

————. *William F. Buckley: Patron Saint of the Conservatives*. Simon & Schuster, 2001.

Klososky, Scott, editor. *The Haldeman Diaries: Inside the Nixon White House*. G.P. Putnam's Sons, 1994.

Lien, Tracey. "Mark Zuckerberg Says Many Conservatives Don't Trust Facebook to Show 'Content Without a Political Bias'." *Los Angeles Times*, May 18, 2016.

Nunez, Michael. "Former Facebook Workers: We Routinely Suppressed Conservative News." *Gizmodo*, May 9, 2016.

Orwell, George. *Facing Unpleasant Facts: Narrative Essays*. Harcourt, Inc., 2008.

Perlstein, Rick. *Nixonland*. Scribner, 2008.

Winik, Jay. *The Great Upheaval: America and the Birth of the Modern World, 1788–1800*. Harper Perennial, 2007.

ABOUT THE AUTHOR

JEFF FLAKE is the junior United States senator from Arizona. He is a fifth-generation Arizonan who was raised on a cattle ranch in Snowflake, a town named in part for his great-great-grandfather. Prior to his election to the U.S. Senate, Flake served in the U.S. House of Representatives from 2001 to 2013, representing the East Valley. Jeff Flake and his wife, Cheryl, live in Mesa and have five children.

Twitter: @JeffFlake
Instagram: @jeffflake

ABOUT THE TYPE

This book was set in Sabon, a typeface designed by the well-known German typographer Jan Tschichold (1902–74). Sabon's design is based upon the original letter forms of sixteenth-century French type designer Claude Garamond and was created specifically to be used for three sources: foundry type for hand composition, Linotype, and Monotype. Tschichold named his typeface for the famous Frankfurt typefounder Jacques Sabon (c. 1520–80).